T0103503

Surfing the
BRAINWAVE

Surfing the BRAINWAVE

HOW I TUNED MY SON'S BRAIN—FOR GOOD!

DR. DICKSON LAI (PHD)

PARTRIDGE

ISBN: Hardcover 978-1-4828-8054-0
Softcover 978-1-4828-8053-3
eBook 978-1-4828-8055-7

Print information available on the last page.

To order additional copies of this book, contact
Toll Free 800 101 2657 (Singapore)
Toll Free 1 800 81 7340 (Malaysia)
orders.singapore@partridgepublishing.com

www.partridgepublishing.com/singapore

Contents

ACKNOWLEDGE

It's been 15 years since I left the country to further my career in other part of the world. It's a great experienced for me in every country I stayed and finally, it's the family that bring me back to home country. It seem that there was an issue yet today, after being through the challenges, I felt problems are opportunities to prepare me to take on bigger thing in life. This book was written for my son, it's heart breaking that I couldn't spend much time with him while I chase for my dream, even today, i am still chasing for my dream... my greatest gratitude goes to 3 special women that make me special. I would like to thank my wife. Her support, encouragement, quiet patience and unwavering love were undeniably the bedrock upon which the past fifteen years of my life have been built. Her tolerance of my occasional vulgar moods is a testament in itself of her unyielding devotion and love. I thank my mother and sister for their faith in me and allowing me to be as ambitious as I wanted. It was under their watchful eye that I gained so much drive and an ability to tackle challenges head on. They have encouraged me to continue my dream and even to pursuit my education. Both of them are strong believer of knowledge and very unfortunate they haven't had chance to pursuit education themselves yet they are self-aware of the important in knowledge.

I started to explore the technology to unleash human brain when I discovered that brain can be re-designed, it all thanks to my mum and sister to have continuously pushing me to explore Brain Activation, because of the clear and detailed explanation by Joyce Chin (Founder of Brain Activation, www.BrainActivation.com.my), who have given me an eye opening analysis, especially the ability to read my son behavior and possible physical wellness. Because of the report that didn't labeled my son ADHD (Hyperactive), that confirmed the opinion from individuals comparing to facts that derived from natural self, in this space is by reading the brainwaves. Due to my curiosity, I literally went out to learn something that i have never thought of, because of that process, i truly believe every human can do wonders as long as there's a determination within. Professor OH Sang-ji (Korea Research Institute of Jungshin Science) who have spend his effort educating and coaching me in the space of Neurofeedback, it was him that I spend literally years to study and researched the possibilities of this hidden technology which has help so many human beings yet it's lag behind in my home country. I was wondering what if we are expose to such methods, we could have created high intelligent society. Wouldn't it be a better place to live in?

I dedicate this book to the world with the earnest hope that it will help us surmount all difficulties and achieve the possibilities surround us.

Chapter One

Miracles from Brain Activation

At the age of 14, William was still in high school, a result of his low intelligence quotient. Having a slow brain and a low level of articulation weren't his only problems; he loved staying on his own, and stayed away from his siblings at home, and away from peers in school.

He forgot things very easily; coupled with the fact that he hardly talks, it showed that his memory retention was very low. The only response he could give to someone was: "I don't know", or to flash a smile.

This was always a source of great worry for his mother and me. You see, when he was younger, he was diagnosed with a hole in the heart, and had to go under surgery to get it corrected. Though the surgery was quite successful, little did we know that his immune response, as well as his brain development, would be affected by the necessary procedure.

As William grew older, there were signs that his brain was not developing normally as he grew. When doing tests, he hardly got any answers correct - no matter how easy the test was. We knew something was wrong, but couldn't lay our finger on what the problem was. Regular reports from his school principal and teachers about his inability to follow the pace of the class in all academic activities were very painful to bear. It wasn't as if he were lazy or not serious with books - the problem seemed to be that he never understood what he was reading. Even when I brought in a private tutor to help him at home, the results were still the same.

It was always heartbreaking each time his teachers called to say that William was not advancing in school. We didn't know how to feel: our own son was as blank as the test sheets that he submitted back. He had no inkling to what the answers to the questions were - or even of what it all meant.

In desperation, we had him examined by different specialists, including some renowned neurosurgeons and psychiatrists. After much consultations and analysis, a psychiatrist had diagnosed as "hyperactive" - which influenced my wife's decision to send him to a special child care home. That made me quite miserable, and I felt hatred for the psychiatrist, whom I felt had unfairly labelled my son without any due medical examinations.

I had already ran out of ideas on what to do to help my kid - so when I learned about the existence of brainwaves and Brain Activation, it gave me a glimmer of hope. I took time to study the several techniques involved, and I learned that a particular brainwave helps with knowledge assimilation. When you are in a lower brainwave state, it is a perfect state for knowledge assimilation. My research led me to discover that the heart surgery that my son had affected his immune responses, resulting in some brain development and functions that kept him at a lower frequency of a lower Brainwave. This meant that knowledge assimilation was almost non-existent, resulting in his brain having only very low retentive abilities.

Brain Activation proved to be very effective in controlling my son's Brainwaves, making them more efficient and resulting in him experiencing improved health condition, better academic performance, and a much more positive view of life. Looking his academic performance these days, it is hard to believe this was the same young man who was termed a dullard and never-do-well by teachers and fellow students alike.

One day, my son came back from school and said to me: "Dad, do you know why I have kept to myself all these years? It's because I have always believed that I never had a suitable reply to whatever questions I was asked - even for the ones I had answers to. I was always more comfortable saying that I didn't know the answer, than facing the mockery of my mates." Now, the situation has changed. My son is back to his normal self, with a very efficient and active brain - all thanks to Brain Activation and Brainwaves.

Human Beings have Different Brainwaves

The idea of different Brainwaves patterns and Brain Activation (also known as Neurofeedback, or NFB) training is not a popular one, even today.

I got to know about Brainwaves from a friend, who has read many books, who gets information from online sources, and who tries to know a little bit about everything. One day we talked about the different levels of knowledge assimilation in people, and what could possibly be responsible for the disparity. She gave me a very surprising answer: that no one was born more intelligent than others; rather, some people develop their brains to be more active than others.

This led to a discussion about my son, and his low level of knowledge assimilation. At that point, she told me that our brains are made up of waves. She said that the states which she assimilates might not be the same states that others assimilate. She gave me a scenario involving two friends from our school days. Chantel and Lilian were roommates who were studying the same course, and they did practically everything together. At the end of their study year, Chantel came out with a First Class Honours, while Lilian came out with a Pass - so people were of the opinion that Chantel had been deceiving Lilian all along. But my knowledge of brainwaves made me understand that Chantel always read using her "assimilated" brainwaves, whereas Lilian read with "non-assimilated" brainwaves.

My friend concluded that the best way to help my son was to find the best brainwaves and get him to stay in that brainwave for longer. From there, I was eager to know more about brainwaves. I searched online, which eventually led to the birth of my career as a life and business coach. I found so much information on brainwaves and NFB that not only was I able help my son, but

I was also able to help people who are struggling - whether in the business or in the academic field - to achieve greater success.

A Quick Look at Brainwaves

The Gamma Brainwave

Known as the fastest of all brainwaves, this brainwave state helps the brain learn faster, get better ideas, learn languages and have more efficient memory processing. It is always present when one is awake, and disappears when one is asleep.

The Beta Brainwave

The second fastest brainwave known. It is always active during the day, and is responsible for feelings of intense alertness, agitation, tension, and fear in people. Most times, people get into this state when they are involved in any kind of mental activity that may arouse the brain.

The Alpha Brainwave

This is the brainwave state the brain goes into when one is calm and relaxed. Its lower frequency makes it lower than the Beta Brainwave. It is known as the "non-arousal" brainwave state, and is attained when one is relaxed after the successful completion of tasks. One who is an Alpha state experiences both physical and mental relaxation, while remaining aware of happenings around him.

The Theta Brainwave

This is the brainwave state used mostly in hypnotherapy, due to its high receptiveness. This is a state of reduced consciousness; mostly, when one is falling asleep, and when waking up from sleep. Tasks carried out under this state are carried out automatically, with neither guilt nor sensation being experienced.

The Delta Brainwave

The Delta Brainwave is known as the slowest of all brainwave states, and produces the lowest frequency waves. This is the state of both unconsciousness, and of deep sleep.

Better Brainwaves for My Son

My son's brainwave level was assessed - and we found out that most of his time is spent on the Theta and Delta states. Conversely, he spent little of his time in the Alpha and Beta states, even though those were the states in which he active most of the time. My son's surgery was what created this imbalance, which affected his knowledge assimilation while he was growing up. All that remained now was to address and fix that imbalance.

That was a delicate task, to say the least. An imbalance can be caused by injury, medication, fatigue, emotional distress, pains, and stress - all of which tends to create a pattern in our brain's activity that is hard to shift. Additionally, brainwave states are such that some will be active in greater frequencies and strengths compared to the others.

There are different ways that we can balance brainwaves. Firstly, our brain activity must match with what we are doing. When in school, for example, a child needs to stay focused and attentive - but when at home, the child will want to relax, resulting in the production of less Beta waves and of more alpha waves.

An individual who gets a physical or emotionally injury which affects the brain will be medically advised to slow down on all activities that require intense brain work, in order for the injured brain to stabilise. However, if the brain stays in that state for too long, it will get stuck in the slower frequencies, and the individual will have difficulty in concentrating, focusing and thinking clearly. This is exactly what happened with my son.

Another important thing is that our brain needs to be able to bounce back from all manner of unhealthy things - particularly, from things that we do to it. In order to achieve this balance in my son's case, NFB training was given to him, which enabled him to maintain a better brainwave pattern.

Activating My Brain NOW

In order to help my son, I contacted a coach about this Brain Activation training, who gave us our training days. On the first day of the training, the coach attached a headband with three gold-plated buttons to my son's forehead. I will never forget that day, and I felt really sorry for my son - but he told me after the training that there was nothing painful at all about the entire process.

My son was placed near a computer - sort of like a television screen - and the coach made him play a brain game, where my son's brain sends out its normal electrical signal to make something happen on the screen. At first, I was very negligent about this: at that time, I couldn't understand how it could possibly help my son get better. To me, it was just like playing a normal video game. However, I came to realise that this was not the case at all; in fact, I was made to understand that the signals that make the desired action happen were the patterns that his brain needed to fall into in order to overcome the problems that my son was struggling with.

After a few weeks of the Brain Activation training, I actually noticed some improvements in his behaviour and academic performance. The signal patterns had started becoming a habit for him, and had been integrated into the way his brain worked. It was a wonderful improvement, and I bought more Brain Activation equipment, as well as increased the number of training sessions from three times a week to five times. The results were amazing and miraculous: within a short time, my son was able to maintain better, more favourable brainwaves - even without the equipment.

Building a Career as a Brain Activation Life & Business Coach

In the process of finding a lasting solution to my son's problems, I discovered the great benefits of Brain Activation treatment, and how it could be used to bring out the best in adults. In my career as a life and business coach, I employed a great deal of Brain Activation techniques, and it has helped change the productivity of my clients in every area of their lives, including their businesses, relationships, and social lives.

Most entrepreneurs and business owners who came to me for help had a similar problem: they were operating under the wrong brainwaves, and - as expected - always ended up with unsatisfactory results. Business owners who consulted with me were able to learn about the different types of brainwaves, and how each could be used to produce the best results.

People occupying different positions in the workplace, or involved in different careers, can make use of different brainwaves. The brainwaves of a technician are different from those of a manager, just as the brainwave of the manager who oversees a certain department of an organisation differs from those of an entrepreneur.

The entrepreneur, by virtue of the great tasks he is saddled with in the running of the business, will have more need of the Gamma Brainwave for peak performance, as the Gamma Brainwave has a very high frequency and is associated with all aspects of idea formation and procession of memory.

Meanwhile, a manager's brain will more often make use of the Alpha Brainwave to ensure peak performance, as this brainwave is responsible for clarity of thoughts, for the making of informed and creative decisions, and for working with less stress and anxiety, among other things. Additionally, a technician's brain in an Alpha state can produce needed results, as his job requires much more relaxed analysis and accurate decisions.

Secrets of NFB

Traditionally, NFB has never been a popular option - but as with everything, this paradigm is slowly changing. In keeping track on NFB developments, it can be seen that NFB is being featured more and more in articles and on programmes by a variety of health magazines and online news sources.

It all leads to a fact that has been known all this while: that this therapy is actually beneficial. According to several studies, NFB can go a long way in improving the functions of the human brain. It can also get rid of problems such as attention deficit disorders and chronic pains. One important fact result of this Brain Activation technique is the ability to perform at peak potential in our daily activities - in our businesses, academics, athletics, or other activities requiring high levels of brain functions.

Equally important is the fact that our "lost potential" can be regained through Brain Activation. When people experience the benefit of this training, they feel a sense of reclaiming their peak potential, once more being able to access the capabilities they have previously experienced. When the brain falls into some patterns, Brain Activation helps to provide the brain with positive encouragement and good feedback.

NFB is used in the treatment of varieties of dysfunctions of the brain such as Attention Deficit Hyperactivity Disorder (ADHD), anxiety, sleep, behavioural problems, headaches, and Post Menopause Syndrome (PMS). It may also be effective for disorders such as seizures and autism. However, it is not really a cure for "disregulations" within the brain; rather, it is an attempt to restore the regular functions of the brain.

Malfunctions that result from these "disregulations" of the brain are fixed over time, as the brain learns to regulate itself. Degenerative diseases - such as Parkinson's and dementia - require long-term treatments, because factors - such as allergies and toxins - may decrease the results of biofeedback over time.

When used as an educational tool, our central nervous system learns to redefine our reactions to stress. The extent of our neurological overreactions and underreactions are reduced, which helps us to be more discerning and to return to a state where we are able to function at our best.

Effects of Brain Activation on Anxiety, Depression and Self-Esteem in Adults

Brain Activation (or NFB) is known to have a lot of benefits in both adults and children, and some of these benefits include self-improvement in adults. Most adults are known to battle with severe cases of anxiety, depression and low self-esteem. The truth about anxiety, depression and low self-esteem is that they are all related, and can lead to poor performance in all areas of life if they are not handled appropriately.

Anxiety, depression and lack of confidence can keep one away from participating in activities that can yield very good dividends and lead to more success in life. People have used many different techniques in an attempt to deal with these issues - and for the majority of them, this has been met with little to no success. Some of the well-known techniques used to treat these cases include therapies, meditation, and hiring a life coach. Of all these, hiring a life coach may be one of the most effective ways to tackle their issues, as most life coaches are known to use different effective techniques to help people issues get better.

One of the most effective techniques used by life coaches to deal with cases of anxiety, depression and lack of confidence is through the use of NFB treatment/training. NFB has been found to be quite effective in treating such cases due to the fact that it is a non-invasive process of monitoring brainwave activities, using a computer that provides feedback to the client. This feedback is used for self-regulation in the areas of controlling thoughts, improving concentration, increasing focus, achieving a more composed and positive mood, as well as for achieving better sleep. All these feedbacks, when utilised for the regulation of different brain activities, go a long way towards reduce anxiety, depression and increasing confidence.

Brain Activation = Neurofeedback

Our brains are self-building, which leaves it susceptible to a whole host of things that can affect it. These include chemical intakes, drugs, or trauma causes, and can damage us at any stage of our lives, whether before birth, or after. Particularly in our formative years, exposure to such effects could lead to our brain creating performance circuits that are very weak, inefficient or even inappropriate for what we want to do in later years.

This can produce serious attention, learning or emotional problems in our later life. Everything can seem to be go on quite well for the child who fell off a slide at age two - until the child starts school and has to sit quietly, or needs to learn to read, or to do math problems. By then, it will be discovered that the minor incident or accident was not so minor after all - and even though it might not be too late, a lot of unnecessary damage has already been done.

The brain problem may multiply itself many times over. As such, even though our brain's strength is in building and re-building itself in a way that causes us to become smarter and more adaptable, physical injuries or difficulties in life may actually cause our brain to make us less bright, more rigid, confused, or even depressed or anxious.

NFB is a natural process that was specifically created to identify and correct brain dysfunctions and "disregulations". With enhanced functions, the brain is better able to maintain itself in a more efficient and resilient state, and we can live in accordance with Nature's original intention: to become wiser and more intelligent, with greater memory and a more resilient mood, as we mature.

The truth about this is that performance, mood, memory, and behaviour are all products of the brain. If you are suffering in any of these areas, it means that your brain is not doing its job as well as it should. These brain disorders can take the form of attention and focus problems (Attention Deficit Disorder); learning difficulties (Learning Disabilities); constant mood patterns (Depression and Anxiety); redundant behaviour (Obsessive-Compulsive Disorder); and seizures (epilepsy) - all examples of the brain doing its job poorly.

It must be noted, however, that not all seizures can be improved using Brain Activation; most of the genetic ones cannot be treated, and neither can the deregulation be reduced. The only difference between these brain disorders is in the place and manner in which the brain is mismanaging its energy. For this, the Quantitative Electroencephalography (QEEG) detects and details the source of the neurological inefficiency. Specific Brain Activation training protocols then assist the brain in healing and repairing itself.

Once done, the symptoms - whether compromised attention, mood, memory, or behaviour - are significantly reduced, or even eliminated altogether. This treatment helps to build peak, elite performance - both athletic and academic - by optimising the brain functions. Because all performance begins and ends in the brain, it follows that when your brain does its job with greater ease and efficiency, your performance must also improve.

A majority of people have reported that after a few sessions of Brain Activation training, they sleep better, often experience an increased sense of peacefulness and report an enhanced level of focus and concentration. Throughout this process, the brain self-regulates and learns where it functions best. It really does work - and at the end of this chapter are several success stories that I am proud to have been able help achieve.

Unleashing the Potential to Gain Peak Performance

During the course of helping people, I am often asked what has become favourite question: "Are we at our peak performance?" "Peak Performance" is easy to recognise - it is the mental state in which you are focused and present, or it can be the point where you are meeting your body's potential in terms of strength and stamina.

As a life and business coach, I have successfully used Brain Activation training to help people achieve their peak performance. This Brain Activation training and treatment is aimed at helping the brain to function at its peak, thereby producing better results. Peak Performance as a result of Brain Activation helps people in different professions to reach the zenith of their different careers, by utilising the power of the brain, where all activities have their roots. Become more articulate and make very informed decisions at all times which ultimately results in much enhanced success.

Many of the common elements of Peak Performance are:

- The ability to focus and attend to tasks;
- Clarity of thought;
- A sense of personal control;
- An absence of self-consciousness;
- A heightened intuition and awareness;
- Appropriate reactions and responses, without struggles;
- Better concentration;
- Better attention spans;
- Ease in decision making;
- A reduced number of errors made;
- A faster response time;
- Enhanced creativity;
- A more efficient memory;
- Accelerated learning;
- An increased immunity to stress;
- Increased productivity;
- A lower susceptibility to burning out;
- Quicker and deeper relaxation;
- Better mind/body integration;
- Enhanced well-being;
- Reduced anxiety and stage fright;
- Increased self-confidence and assertiveness;
- Better self-control;
- Development of self-awareness; and
- Development of emotional intelligence.

Sports People and the Peak Performance State

One of such profession that greatly benefits from this Brain Activation training is that of sports. The men and women who have undergone this training have experienced a more increased efficiency in their performance, as their brains are able to help them stay more focused and coordinated while they train and compete. With this training, these sportsmen are able to think more clearly. Sportsmen are increasingly using brain-training techniques to improve focus and screen out distractions

The Feeling of Greatness

In my years as a life and business coach, I have used Brain Activation to help people of different ages and races get their brain power. Below are some success stories of my patients who have used Brain Activation to get their brains functioning at maximum capacity, and to articulate themselves more accurately (In the interest of patient confidentiality, the names of the patients - and their parents/guardians - have been removed):

- One 45-year-old engineer has said that the Brain Activation training has helped him understand the neurological basis for his attention-related limitations, as well as the role that his previously prescribed medications had in reducing them. He said that the training has enhanced his performance. "Not only was the training helpful and educative, but it gave me much fun as well," he said.
- The parents of a restless 8-year-old boy have said that Brain Activation helped calm their restless and aggressive son. According to them, he displayed abnormal behaviour for someone his age, escalating and act it out at home and at school, where he always seemed to be out of control. They happily reported that after he went through the training session, he is behaving better - with testimonies from his teachers, counsellors, his friends' parents, who say that he is easier to be with now, especially at birthday parties and all other outdoor events. "He listens more, he is friendlier, more confident, and able to sit at a place

for longer periods without making a mess," his parents said. "He gets into less trouble while at home. We are grateful for how they have worked with our son to achieve this feat."

- The mother of a teenager used to complain that her son caused so many problems: he always losses focus, has no patience when doing things, and has very low self-esteem. At the beginning of the training, she was sceptical as to what the results will possibly be - but to her surprise and delight, the results exceeded all of her expectations. Now, she is pleased with the whole processes that her son has gone through. He is more focused now, more relaxed, more patient, and his self-esteem has greatly improved. Perhaps best of all is that his life no longer revolves around his medication.
- A 60-year-old mother, grandmother and business owner said that after her training, she is now better both at finding words and at articulation. "I am better at organising and structuring, both at work and at home," she said. She now takes on tasks that were once overwhelming. Although she still takes medication, she says that her focus and creativity are better NFB. "I can now follow through on my ideas, and turn the abstract into a finished product," she noted.
- The mother of a 9-year-old boy professed that this training has helped her son to be become less aggressive at home, and that he is in more control of his actions.
- A 13-year-old boy reported that NFB has helped him to be able to finish long math assignments. "It is easier to finish school work that is boring and hard," he said. "My anxiety attacks have gone from once a week to once a month. I am more comfortable eating lunch in the lunchroom at school, and talking to other kids. I used to eat lunch in the school office."
- A 47-year-old schoolteacher of 25 years said that his anxiety in social situations is hardly noticeable anymore, and that he is now able to take situations as they come instead of getting anxious about what might happen - both at work and in social situations.
- A 10-year-old boy said that he now listens better at school, and can sit still longer when doing something boring. This is unlike before, as he used to yell whenever he got frustrated at school.

- An elite figure skater said that this training has helped her so much with her skating. She said that she is now more able to hit her jumps, and does not have a million thoughts going through her head while it happens.
- A 10-year-old boy has benefited from this training, his 4th-grade teacher reported. "The student now shows more focus, and is attacking work more on his own - which is wonderful!" the teacher said. "He is less and less frustrated with his work, is more concerned about getting his work finished, and he is more responsible with the routine." The teacher said that the student has moved into a more challenging math group, where he is engaged and likes to listen and participate.
- A 72-year-old highly-educated grandmother has reported that the training has helped her to be more focused, and that she gets more work done by herself. She added that she is much less depressed than she was before she started the training.

Marrie's Amazing Story

This is a report given by Marrie, on how Brain Activation has helped her son learn self-control":

> "When my son turned four, it was as if a switch had been flipped. His quiet, dreamy, observant, and laid-back manner was replaced with one that howled, kicked, scratched, bit, and was opposed to everything. Everything normal that you would do with children that was expected became a battle, from getting dressed in the morning to brushing his teeth at night.
>
> "By the time my son had his seventh birthday, we saw little improvement - and it was clear that this was not a developmental issue that would go away. He was sent home from pre-school on numerous occasions for hurting other children; it got so bad that he was suspended. The impact of all this was wearing me down - and I was constantly compromising my parenting, lest my

request for him to pick up his bath towel would turn into a hostage negotiation. The most disturbing issue was the fact that he never remember his tantrums once they were over - he often acted as though nothing had even happened. I knew it was not an act - and I knew I had to do something.

"I first learned about Brain Activation from a close friend, who had sent her adopted son for treatment - with great success. It was not until I was interviewed with Dickson that I learned of the term 'emotional disregulation', and how it applied to my son. I was intrigued by the articles he gave me to read on the subject, and by the testimonials from those who had experienced dramatic results. Although I was sceptical that it could help my son, I was entirely hopeful.

"What appealed to me the most about the programme was that for those it helped, the impact was usually permanent. The goal of Brain Activation is to train the brain to correct its own responses and optimise itself in situations where previously it could not get itself out of park. Dickson said this when he was trying to explain this in layman's terms. He said that the feedback would help my son's brain choose a new response, and recognise the association between cause and effect. This would, in turn, enable my son to regulate himself when faced with situations that would formerly make him escalate out of control.

"Over the course of our time with Dickson, I saw my son's oppositional pilot control of 'No, I won't, and you can't make me do it!' begin to mellow into something that sounded much more like a typical 7-year-old's reluctance son to comply. He would sometimes say: 'Oh, man!' when I ask him to clear his dinner plate, while doing it anyway with a sheepish grin.

"It's been six months of Brain Activation, and we are in the homestretch. I have seen a dramatic improvement in my son's behaviour, and his general mood seems happy and easy going. It is in the complete contrast with the brooding boy who used to be so easily triggered. I am thrilled with the results, and have tremendous gratitude and hope that those who suffer with other disorders can gain the help they need."

Having just been diagnosed with attention deficit disorder herself, Marrie said that she has started her own Brain Activation training, having recently learned that Brain Activation can correct a host of other disorders. "My own Brain Activation training has also helped me to achieve normalcy!"

Chapter Two

Neurofeedback (NFB)

Neurofeedback (NFB) is a technique used to improve the brain's ability to operate more successfully. Arising from the field of psychology rather than medicine, it actually involves an individual taking responsibility for his or her own conditions, and in participating actively in it. The technique is also known by several names: neurotherapy, neurobiofeedback, electroencephalography (EEG) neurofeedback and EEG biofeedback.

NFB is a computer-aided training method, in which selected parameters of the client's own brain activity - which cannot be perceived or seen - are made visible to the patient. The individual sees or hears what the brain is doing at the moment - the feedback - through a monitor and loudspeaker.

Through the feedback that the clients get, they learn how to regulate their brain activity in order to overcome many illnesses that are due to "disregulation" of brain activity, thus achieving better functionality. Positive feedback is generated for desired brain activity, with negative feedback generated for undesired brain activity. Hence, the brain patterns are continuously monitored, providing a feedback loop. NFB can be said to be a type of biofeedback, using precise instruments to measure brainwaves to provide real-time display and feedback on brain activity which can be used for self-regulation.

NFB reads brain patterns and provides a way to "exercise" and challenge our brain's performance. In the same way that maintaining physical fitness requires constant practices by doing physical exercises, maintaining mental fitness is also applicable to the brain, which is where NFB - which has also been called neurotherapy - comes in.

As a technique used to improve the brain's abilities and to make you operate more successfully, NFB first measures the brain's electrical patterns, through small sensors that are embedded into an adjustable visor. These electrical patterns are processed by special devices that allow visual display or auditory feedback of these signals, through the use of video games or DVD movies.

For example: assume you are playing a game with full concentration, all your mind and senses are alert (in other words, the desired brain state). You will see yourself taking absolute control of the game, and winning the game. But when you are not in the desired state, you will find out that you are losing, your speed and your control over the game will decrease.

Imagine you are subway surfing - knowing fully well that you are being followed; knowing that whenever you hit a train, you will be caught. When playing this kind of game, full concentration is needed so that you will not be hit by the train. You notice that as you improve your focus, your speed increases and also your stage.

As your stage gets higher, so does your brain state - because more concentration is needed, and the player needs to be alert. Even though this involves video games, the same thing applies with DVD media player systems. The brain signals pass through a computer receiver, affecting the size of the movie screen and the volume. The more you pay attention and channel your brain towards it, the more you see and hear while the movie is playing. But when your thoughts are far from the movie you are playing, you will find it difficult to hear - let alone understand - the movie.

We can also take the example of a person who cannot stand. When made to stand with the aid of an object (say, a walking stick) before a mirror, he is made to say to himself: "I can really stand!" With this in his mind, he can be guided to continue making practices - with the eventual result that he can achieve his aim of standing without using any aids.

The consistent use of NFB brain exercises can help to strengthen and reinforce the brain; it can lead to increased awareness and differentiation of mental states; it naturally empowers the brain's neuro-plasticity, and ability to think more clearly; it helps you pay attention for longer periods without getting tired; it aids you in retaining facts and improving your memory.

A Brief History of NFB

In the year 1924, electric currents were detected in human brain by German psychiatrist Hans Berger, who connected a couple of electrodes to a patient's scalp and detected the currents using a ballistic galvanometer. He was expanding on work previously conducted on animals by Richard Caton, who had worked on the exposed cerebral hemispheres of rabbits and monkeys, and discovered electrical phenomena.

After this discovery, Berger carried out more research to back up his observations, eventually inventing the electroencephalogram (from which we get the term EEG). During the year 1929-1938, he analysed EEGs qualitatively, and published 14 reports about studies on EEGs. However, it was his assistant G. Dietch who in 1932 became the first researcher on quantitative EEG, through his application of Fourier analysis to seven EEG records.

NFB was popularised by Joe Kamiya, a professor in the University of Chicago. In 1968, he published an article about the Alpha Brainwave experiment that he had been conducting in the early 1960s. In his experiment, he trained volunteers to recognise and alter their Alpha Brainwave activity. His experiment was in two parts:

In the first part, the volunteer was asked to keep their eyes closed at the sound of a tone, and they say whether he thought he was in Alpha.

In the second stage, he asked the subjects from his study to go into Alpha at the sound of a bell and not to go into the state when it rang twice.

It was noticed that at first stage, 50% of the respondents were correct. At the second stage, some subjects were able to go into the state on command, while others could not control it. The results were significant, and very attractive. Kamiya later published a paper with James Hardt that demonstrated the efficacy of EEG biofeedback training.

Five years after Kamiya's experiment, Barry Sterman conducted a revolutionary study on cats at the behest of the National Aeronautics and Space Administration (NASA) of the USA. His experiment proved that cats that had been trained to consciously alter their sensorimotor rhythm were resistant to doses of hydrazine, which typically induced seizures. This finding was applied to humans in 1971, when Sterman trained an epileptic to control her seizures through a combination of sensorimotor rhythm and EEG neurotherapy. These very miraculous findings allowed the epileptic to obtain a driver's license after only three months of treatment.

Around the same time, Hershel Toomim founded the Toomim Biofeedback Laboratories and Biocomp Research Institute, on the basis of a device known as the Alpha Pacer, which measured brain waves. After working for decades with various biofeedback mechanisms, Toomim accidentally stumbled upon conscious control of cerebral blood flow in 1994. He developed a device specific to this measure, which he called a Near Infrared Spectrophotometry Hemencephalography (NIR HEG) system, coining the term hemoencephalography in 1997. Later, Jeffrey Carmen - a clinician user of NIR HEG - adapted Toomim's system for migraines in 2002, by integrating peripheral thermal biofeedback into the design. Since then, both techniques have been applied to numerous disorders of frontal and prefrontal lobe function.

The Questions I Asked

After I decided to become a life and business coach and dove deeper into the world of brainwaves and NFB, I found myself asking several questions that I know I needed the answers to, in order to be a more effective coach. These are the questions that I asked, and that I found answers for.

How does NFB work?

NFB works by applying an electrode to the scalp, which is connected to a computer. The signal is processed in the computer, and certain information about the key brainwave frequencies are extracted. The flow of this brainwave activity is shown back to the person, who attempts to change the activity level. Here, the person sees some frequencies which he wishes to promote, as well as others that he wishes to diminish. This information is presented to the person in the form of a video game. As the person is effectively playing the video game with his or her brain, the brainwave activity is eventually shaped towards a more desirable and more regulated performance. At this point, the frequencies we target - and the specific locations on the scalp where we listen in on the brain - are specific to the conditions we are trying to address, and specific to the individual.

Who Provides NFB?

NFB can be provided by everyone, even those who have little or no knowledge of it. The only thing you need to do is just follow the instructions on how to play the video game, using only your brain waves. However, it can be provided by professional mental health professionals such as coaches, psychologists, family therapists, and counsellors. The training may also be provided by nurses, clinical social workers, rehabilitation specialists, by Medical Doctors or by trained staff (if the above-mentioned professionals are not available). These professions usually work with clients on a one-on-one basis, in order to know the exact problems of the patient, as well as the root of their problems. With the information which the client gains from these professionals, he or she can practice the brainwave exercises on their own, by attaching passive sensors to the scalp with the EEG paste, which then pick up brain waves. A computer processes the brainwaves and extracts certain information from them. The flow of brainwaves is shown to the client in the form of a video game, and the client is then instructed on how to play the video game using only specific brainwaves. These sensors are painless, and does not involve the application of any voltage or electric currents to the brain.

Does NFB provide a permanent Cure?

No. NFB is not really a cure in the case of organic brain disorders. It can only be a matter of getting the brain to function better, as opposed to curing the condition permanently. The good news is that almost any brain - regardless of its functional level - can be trained to function better, which is achieved by greater frequency of training. NFB trains the brain to regulate itself. When it comes to problems of "disregulation", self-regulation may be the remedy because it is not a disease to be cured. As such, the word "cure" would not apply. The greatest benefit of NFB is that once you have completed the training, the effects are permanent. Once the brain has been regulated, there are very few instances that can reverse the positive changes of training. For example, severe trauma to the head or severe emotional trauma can sometimes hinder the effects of the training.

Do the Training Effects Last?

Yes - with reference to the previous question - when the problem being addressed is one of brain "disregulation". NFB involves learning by the brain, and if that brings order out of disorder, the brain will continue to use its new capabilities - thus, reinforcing them. However, when dealing with degenerative conditions or when working against continuing stresses to the system (as is the case of the autism spectrum), the training needs to be continued at some level over time, in order to yield positive results. For instance, a child living in a toxic environment will have more difficulty retaining good functions; hence, more training or longer training time would be required in this kind of state.

What about Medication?

With successful NFB training, the medications targeting brain functions may be needed at lower dosages - or even no longer necessary - because the brain takes over the role of regulating itself more and more. This decreased dependency is particularly striking when the medications play a supportive role in any event, as has always been the case for more severe disorders. The important thing here is that clients should communicate with their prescribing physician regarding NFB and medications. It is best not to start NFB if you are also starting medication or changing dosages - that way, you can actually tell which treatment is the one that is actually working.

Are there any Side Effects of using NFB?
Studies have shown no side effects of NFB purely because nothing is put into the body or brain - the process is very gentle, and no force is applied. In actual fact, most people feel more relaxed and alert after a session - and because of this, the brain tends to move toward balance and equilibrium. However, some brains are more sensitive than others, and anything that can help can also potentially cause a problem. Emotions might bubble up as your brain begins to process them, or there might be a temporary response that is stronger. These effects fade as you get used to the process. A licensed and experienced practitioner can adjust the feedback to make changes to address these things, or look ahead and prevent them from happening anyway.

Who uses the technique?

Adult and children of all ages have had great success with NFB training. NFB can help a variety of childhood problems which includes the following:

- Bedwetting;
- Nightmares;
- Night Terrors;
- Sleepwalking; and
- Teeth Grinding.

NFB can assist adolescents and adults who are either struggling with the following disorders:

- Anxiety;
- Depression;
- Learning Disabilities;
- Epilepsy;
- Substance Abuse;
- Seizures;
- Attention Deficit Disorders (ADD/ADHD);
- Autism;

- Sleep Disorders (Insomnia);
- Fibromyalgia;
- Chronic Pain;
- Irritable Bowel Syndrome;
- Weight Issues;
- Post-Traumatic Stress Disorder (PTSD); and
- Strokes/Traumatic Brain Injuries.

Attention Deficit Hyperactivity Disorder (ADHD)

ADHD is the most common neurobehavioral disorder in children, affecting nearly five percent of the population. About 25% of children out of the millions treated with ADHD medication may not respond to treatment or cannot tolerate the side effects of the medication. Patients with ADHD have an "under-aroused" brain, with insufficient communication among the neurons. NFB protocols - which is based on the relationship between BrainWave frequencies and mental state - have been developed to inhibit cortical slowing, and to normalise the EEG activity in the area which is supposed to control attention and behaviour. In the form of a rewards system, the patient learns to enhance the EEG "desired" frequencies and suppress the "undesired" ones.

ADHD has also been a focus of HEG research. Some authors claim that research into NFB has been limited, and that it is of low quality. Some argued that there is some indication on the effectiveness of biofeedback for ADHD, but that it is not conclusive. A more recent review concluded that standard neurofeedback protocols for ADHD - such as theta/beta, SMR and slow cortical potentials NFB - are well investigated, and have demonstrated specificity, with no serious adverse side effects from NFB being reported.

QEEG has been used to develop EEG models of ADHD. Persons with ADHD often have too many slow Theta brainwaves that are associated with relaxation, and not enough fast Beta brainwave activities that are associated with mental focus. NFB therapies for ADHD generally attempt to increase the production of Beta Waves, and decrease the number of slower brainwaves. This can be accomplished by allowing the patient to view their levels of brainwaves on a screen and getting them to attempt to alter them. Alternatively, it can be done by integrating brainwaves into a video game.

In one typical case study, an adolescent with ADHD presented highly abnormal QEEG readings and "attentional" scores on neuropsychological tests. After only ten HEG training sessions, he rendered a completely normal QEEG reading, and significantly improved scores on "attentional" measures. The improvements persisted for eighteen months post-treatment, allowing the patient to greatly reduce the drug therapy necessary for him to function successfully, thus offering a quick and relatively cheap treatment alternative for adults with ADD/ADHD.

Anxiety

Anxiety can take many forms: excessive worrying; a nagging sense of fear; negative thinking; and defensiveness. When feeling anxious, your heart races, your hands sweat, you might feel difficulty in breathing, and you might also feel restless or overly emotional. Anxiety sufferers are often overwhelmed, exhausted, and stressed out. Some cannot even concentrate, due to the intense internal focus that they feel. Others obsess about certain things.

NFB is a powerful tool for reducing anxiety and panic attacks, because even with medications, anxiety stills persists. Medication only reduces symptoms - and sometimes has side effects when the patient stops taking the medication. This is because they might have gotten used to the medication, and have developed a dependency for it. Additionally, medication does not teach new and healthier patterns - rather, it promotes a lack of self-awareness. NFB has proven to be an alternative to medication that helps people by eliminating or reducing their need for drug to counter anxiety; thus, their brains become more stable.

Brain training NFB is not all about training you to manage your stress - it also helps to treat the part of your brain that controls stress. When people are dealing with anxiety, part of their brain is simply not doing its job of keeping them calm. NFB comes into play when trying to change part of that brain that is not doing its job well, with Biofeedback the quickest and fastest way to teach you how to help yourself.

The way to use NFB to treat anxiety utilises what is called Brain Mapping. Brain Mapping helps you identify the problematic areas of your brain, and helps to target the NFB treatments to the area that need it the most. For example, if the recording of an EEG for a client showed an excessively fast brain pattern, her brain activity can be measured and a better computer game will be given to the client to help train her brain to calm down. With the proper amount of training, the brain learns to maintain healthier patterns to correct anxiety.

Epilepsy

Epilepsy is a long-term neurological disorder, characterised by epileptic seizures. These seizures vary from brief and nearly undetectable episodes, to long period of vigorous shaking. Seizures tend to occur in epilepsy, and it has no immediate underlying cause. Epilepsy cannot be cured - but seizures are controllable, with the proper medication. However, it has been found that about one third of patients with epilepsy do not benefit from medical treatment. For these patients, EEG Biofeedback is a viable alternative. Not all cases of epilepsy are life long, and a substantial number of people show improvement, to the extent that medication is no longer needed. Meta-analysis carried out by Tan et al. in 2009 identified 63 studies on NFB for the treatment of epilepsy, where the analysis showed a small effect size for treatment.

Depression

Depression is a state of low mood and aversion to activity that can affect a person's thoughts, behaviour, feeling and sense of well-being. A depressed person can feel sad, anxious, empty, hopeless, worried, helpless, worthless, guilty, irritable, hurt or restless. A depressed mood is not always a psychiatric disorder, though, and may just be a normal reaction to certain life events. Studies by Linden et al on NFB with functional magnetic resonance imaging used on eight patients with major depressive disorders showed that the NFB section resulted in the "upregulation" of the brain areas which were shown to be involved in the generation of positive emotions.

Insomnia

Insomnia is a sleep disorder in which there is an inability to either fall asleep or to stay asleep as long as desired, and is particularly common in elderly people. EEG Biofeedback has demonstrated its effectiveness in the treatment of insomnia, with improvements in duration of sleep as well as quality of sleep. Stimulus control therapy is a treatment for patients who have conditioned themselves to associate the bed, or sleep, with a negative response. Stimulus control therapy involves taking steps to control the sleep environment. A component of this is sleep restriction, a technique that aims at matching the time spent in bed with the actual time spent asleep. This technique involves maintaining a strict sleep-wake schedule: sleeping only at certain times of the day, and for specific amounts of the time, in order to induce mild sleep deprivation. Meditation has been recommended for the treatment of insomnia, because it helps to produces relaxation and sound sleep. NFB training reduces "wake-after-sleep" onsets, and increases total sleep time.

Migraines

A migraine is a type of severe headache that is often accompanied with vomiting and difficulty in seeing. A four-year study of 100 chronic migraine sufferers found that after 30-minute training sessions (which took place an average of six times), 90% of patients reported significant improvements with their migraines. Another study conducted combined the Biofeedback measures of EEG and thermal handwarming during thrice-weekly sessions for 14 months. A reduction in the migraines of at least 50% was experienced by 70% of sufferers, following combined neurotherapy and drug treatments, as opposed to 50% for those undergoing only traditional drug therapy, without the use of NFB.

Peak Performance

It has been assumed that the underlying cause for a variety of disorders is a "disregulation" of brain functions and enhancing peak performance in normal adults. The aim of an NFB session is to train the brain towards better functionality, after which the brain is supposed to adopt the improved function, leading to the symptoms of the disorder diminishing.

People who are already high performers - like musicians, athletes and top business executives who want to become better in their field - use NFB to achieve peak performance in what they do.

NFB is also used successfully for deep relaxation and meditation, where people with migraines have excellent success relieving themselves of their migraines and discontinuing their medications forever. Individuals suffering from autism have had their lives dramatically changed, as well as experiencing a higher quality of life with the entire family. People who have been diagnosed with ADD or ADHD have had enormous success with NFB. With the elderly, regular NFB training can possibly support good brain functionality. Independent of the current state of the brain, almost all brains can be trained towards better functionality.

All that needs to be noted is that NFB is not a universal remedy for some of the above-mentioned disorders, and cannot always replace medication.

Successful Cases of NFB Use Worldwide

Scientists have registered a tremendous number of success stories on the use of NFB in treating the above-mentioned disorders. Some former migraine sufferers report that they have not had a migraine for several years, after the use of NFB. Another study shows that NFB therapy of attention deficits (ADD/ADHD) can lead to similar results as a therapy with Methylphenidate (also known as Ritalin). For patients that take medication for specific disorders, NFB treatment has been proven to help reduce or even discontinue the need for medication.

Clinicians and researchers who have had more than twenty years of experience using NFB had studied the effects - both academically and scientifically - and have published the positive results in numerous peer-reviewed journals. There is a significant body of research regarding benefits in the treatment of ADHD, as mentioned. More recently, researchers are investigating the use of NFB for Autism Spectrum Disorders, due to promising emerging results. Other than its more medical applications, NFB has also been used successfully for deep relaxation and meditation.

The fact that NFB can help people even extends to the arts in fields such as music, dance, and acting, where users have managed to enhance their performances. A study found that a form of Biofeedback produced benefits in dance, by enhancing performance in competitive ballroom dancing, and increasing cognitive creativity in contemporary dancers. NFB has also been shown to instil a superior flow state in actors, possibly due to greater immersion while performing.

Some results showed that among the vast majority of clients who have had an experience with NFB, greater than 95% have an actual outcome that exceeds the prior expectations, in one clinician's experience. The changes that can be produced with NFB can be said to be miraculous. One EEG Biofeedback office has a sign on its front desk: "We expect miracles. If none occur, something has gone wrong." What appears to be miraculous in all of this is really nothing more than the incredible capacity of our brains to recover functionality when given the chance.

The Pros and Cons of NFB

There are plenty of arguments given by experts on both sides of the NFB divide. Proponents believe that NFB should be part of an adult's ADHD treatment plans for the following reasons:

- NFB does not require use of drugs, and is a non-invasive procedure - hence, it may be used by adults who may not be able to tolerate ADHD drugs, or who have a history of substance abuse.
- NFB is ideal for ADHD adults who do not like taking stimulant medications, which they fear may alter their personality or disrupt their natural talents or creativity, turning them into a pale and boring shadow of themselves. Adults with facing this problem with stimulants find NFB to be a fun, exciting, and interesting experience; in some

cases, NFB may even be as effective as stimulants, without having significant side effects.

- Proponents of NFB claim to have a solid record of treating a variety of conditions, including adult ADHD. They say that NFB has been a successful intervention in modifying seizures, traumatic brain injury, chronic pain, autistic behaviours, migraines, depression, anxiety, addictions, and sleep problems. In addition, it has also been used to resolve reading and math disability, and has reportedly helped famous athletes, artists, top business people, and executives achieve peak performance.
- Proponents of NFB have also said that some ADHD adults enjoy long-lasting positive changes, increased self-confidence and self-esteem, reduced negative behaviour and negative thinking patterns and more after undergoing NFB training.
- The majority of patients completing treatment reportedly show marked improvement in brainwave functions, because the right criteria are used to select candidates for therapy and treatment, by getting to know their problems and selecting the right NFB measures for them.

Those who oppose the validity of NFB believe that it should be approached with caution for the following reasons:

- There is not enough conclusive scientific evidence to show that it really works. Unlike most ADHD medications, NFB is expensive because of constant practice/constant use - and for each usage, the therapist has to be paid.
- Some opponents said that NFB is very time consuming - unlike drugs, which will not take even a second to consume.
- NFB benefits are not long-lasting. Proponents who argue this believe that the disorders could occur again after a stop.
- Finally, they argue that the effects of NFB are not that fast, and may take about 30 sessions for the desired effects to kick in.

People Who Gain the Most from NFB

Individuals of any age can benefit from NFB training, especially individuals who want to unleash their potential to gain Peak Performance. It is sad to note that even though this is a great technology, NFB is mostly used by children because of disorder symptoms, which neglects the fact that it can have a great impact on anyone who wants a breakthrough.

Anyone who is diagnosed with ADHD that has between above-average and below-average intelligence can be improved with NFB. Most of the above-mentioned disorders - migraine, epilepsy, seizure, depression, anxiety, etc. - are mostly found in adults. In essence, adults need NFB much more than adolescents and children. NFB can assist adolescents who struggle with anxiety, depression or drug and/or alcohol use. And although children need NFB for issues such as bedwetting, nightmares, night terrors, sleepwalking and teeth grinding, these are still not as great a need that those suffered by adults. This is borne out by the fact that you hear of cases where children are hospitalised just because they are bedwetting or have nightmares. In summary, NFB can help anyone maintain good brain function as they age.

Short- and Long-Term Benefits

Short-Term Benefits, as stated by proponents of NFB, include:

- Improved attention spans;
- Improved focus and concentration;
- An increase in organisational skills;
- An increase in the ability to complete tasks; and
- A reduction in impulsivity and hyperactivity.

Long-Term Benefits include:

- Improved behaviour at home, at work, and in social settings;
- Improved aptitude when learning and mastering new skills;

- Higher intelligence test scores;
- Increased self-esteem, confidence, and social poise;
- Improved job performance;
- Increased financial stability;
- Higher socioeconomic status;
- Improved health;
- Increased mental and emotional stability;
- Better marital relationships (which could also lead to a lower divorce rate);
- More stable relationships with friends, colleagues, peers, and bosses; and
- Greater realisation of innate potentials that can be wide-reaching and affect virtually every aspect of an individual's life.

Why NFB is Not Popular

Though NFB has been written about in magazines and journals, it has not yet gained acceptance by the American Medical Association. This single fact alone could be the reason why NFB is not yet acknowledged in the medical world. In earlier times, NFB was adjudged by many as unsafe and ineffective, due to studies that have seem to make it unpopular for so long. However, going by the number of people who have researched on this all-important topic, as well as by the number of books, journals and articles that have been written on it, NFB is gradually growing in popularity, and gaining wider acceptance.

Although NFB is still not thoroughly acknowledged in the field of medicine - where treatments with NFB are normally not covered by health insurance - it is developing very rapidly, because there seems to be an increasing demand for therapeutic services, coupled with the fact that the necessary power and high-technology has become relatively cheaper in the last years. There are also more good training courses and comprehensible programmes methods that are available today compared to before - and the unfavoured status of NFB may change yet.

Chapter Three
Brainwaves are Neural Oscillations

The Meaning of Brainwaves

It is a known fact that our brain is an electrochemical organ comprising of a tight network of nerve cells, all interacting with one another. This interaction results in the generation of an electric field, which is detectable with using standard medical equipment.

These billions of nerve cells - called neurons - use electricity to communicate with each other, and the resulting combination of signals produces an enormous amount of electrical activity in the brain. A brainwave can be said to be the combination of the brain's electrical activity, or as the superposition of the multitude of electrical states being formed by your nervous system. These activities appear in a cyclic, wave-like manner, which is why it is called a "wave".

This electric field is present not only in the brain, but wherever there is a nerve cell. As such, our entire body has an electric field - although it must be said that it is more concentrated around our heads purely because that is where the bulk of the nerve cells are. The simplest proof that we all possess an electric field can be seen each time we feel an electric shock, whether static or otherwise.

Since our brain comprises of a tight network of nerve cells which interact with one another and generate an enormous electrical field, all the overlying electrical patterns that comprise our brainwaves are governed by the same equations that govern the electromagnetic spectrum, including light and particles.

Our thoughts are formed in the brain's electrical field - and this can be measured by hooking up a few wires from your head to a machine. In a sense, it means that our thoughts are governed by the same rules of quantum mechanics and Schrödinger energy wave equations - all of the things in quantum mechanics that describe how an electron or photon behaves.

The major difference between humans and photons are: we can think; we are conscious; we can affect our environment, since we are entangled in it; and we can influence the randomness, just as it can influence us. Our minds are able to receive and send signals into the quantum soup of the zero point field, by way of the highly-coherent frequencies of our thoughts. The higher the frequency of our thoughts/brainwaves, the higher our consciousness. The level of our consciousness is what makes our reality what it is, and what it will continue to be.

The electrical activity in the brain can be detected using sensitive medical equipment, such as an electroencephalogram (EEG), which measures electricity levels over the area of the scalp. The brainwave is represented with a normal wave diagram below.

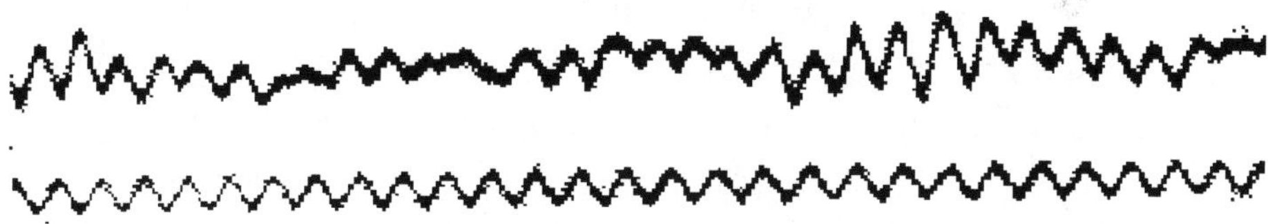

The science of brainwaves came with the discovery that electrical activity in the brain will change, depending on what the person is thinking. For example, the brain wave of someone who is awake is vastly different from the brainwave of someone who is sleeping. Our brain respond to stimuli (regulates its activities) by means of electrical waves - which are registered in the brain - that emit electronic impulses, in waves of varying frequencies that can be registered on an EEG. The stimuli can come from any area of our lives, be it emotional, physical or environmental.

The various levels of brainwave frequencies detected, arranged in their order of frequency (from the most activity to the least) are as follows:

- **Gamma brainwaves** - Gamma brainwaves have a relatively low amplitude and very high frequency, ranging from 27Hz and above. It is the fastest of all the five different brainwaves, because of its high frequency and small wavelength. It is associated with various types of learning, formation of ideas, language and memory processing. This wave disappears during deep sleep, and reappears in a wakeful state.
- **Beta brainwaves** - These are of relatively low amplitude and high frequency, ranging from 12Hz-27Hz. It is second in terms of frequency speed. Beta Waves are a characteristic of a strongly-engaged mind, which is the mental state that most people are in during the day, i.e. when they are awake. In this state, we are consciously alert, and we may feel agitated, tense and afraid. Our brains produce Beta waves when we are in a state of heightened watchfulness and reactivity. It was noted by Berger that aggressive behaviour may erupt when we are in the Beta state, when our brains are aroused and actively engaged in mental activities. Examples of people in this state include someone having an active conversation; a pastor preaching in a church; or someone giving a talk in a programme. The importance of this state should not be underestimated, because many people lack sufficient Beta wave activity, which can cause mental or emotional disorders (such as depression). Stimulating Beta wave activity can improve emotional stability, concentration, attentiveness and the energy level in persons. The Beta sub range (or SMR), which has a frequency range of 12Hz-15Hz, has almost the same characteristics as that of the Beta. There is also consciousness in this state, where insufficient SMR could lead to insomnia.
- **Alpha brainwaves** - This kind of brainwave is produced under calm conditions, when we are relaxed. It has a higher amplitude than that of the Beta wave, but has a shorter frequency that ranges from 8Hz-12Hz. Alpha brainwaves are slower than Beta brainwaves because of its lower frequency. Alpha waves is represented as the "non-arousal"

state, because a person enters an Alpha wave state after completion of a task, where he is in a state of physical and mental relaxation (although his is still aware of what is happening around him). It is a state that occurs naturally both when you just get up from sleep, and when you close your eyes before falling asleep - the closing of the eyes in this instance is a trigger for the brain to automatically produce more Alpha waves. In this state, people will take time to reflect and meditate - to recall memories, feel less discomfort and pain, and also feel a reduction in stress and anxiety. It follows, then that when we are in this state, we naturally have a better command of life, health, and mood. Our thoughts are very clear, and we make more creative decisions. Scientists have found that the people who frequently achieve an Alpha wave state tend to be more creative than people who do not.

- **Theta brainwaves** - This wave has a higher amplitude and lower frequency, ranging from 3Hz-8Hz. This wave is a very receptive mental state, which has proven useful for hypnotherapy. In this state, we are still conscious, yet in the deepest state of relaxation: a state of reduced consciousness. We are in the Theta state as we fall asleep, and as we gradually awaken. Here, tasks become so automatic that you can mentally disengage from them. Ideas that take place in this state often flow and freely, and occur without sensation or guilt.
- **Delta brainwaves** - This is the slowest type of brainwave because of its higher amplitude. The waves produced here are at the lowest frequency, ranging from 0.2Hz-3Hz. In this state, the person is unconscious, or in a deep sleep.

Thinking Beta is Better, While Not Knowing that Alpha is the Best

We might think that being in the Beta state is much more important than others, because that state sharpens our responses and keeps us alert. However, although the Beta state is important, the long term effect of operating in the Beta state could be destructive without the individual noticing it.

Being in this state can make us edgy and stressed out, and some people may suffer negative psychological and physical side effects as a result of spending much time in the Beta state. It must be noted that decisions made in the Beta state are sometimes reactive and defensive, as opposed to being collaborative and constructive when in the Alpha state.

The summary of these brainwaves is somewhat rotational - a form of transition, ranging from your state of wakefulness all the way to the sleeping one. It has been found that we are always in different states, moving from Gamma to Delta, with the brain producing a number of chemical hormones that have a pronounced effect on our moods, productivity and general health.

Brainwaves and Daily Activities

Throughout the day, we shift through different levels of brainwave activity. When you are asleep, you are deep in Delta; your body and mind are relaxed; your unconsciousness lets you dream, assimilate information, play with ideas and explore options freely.

When the cock crows, you hear the sound, thinking you are dreaming but still relaxing on bed - you are now in a Theta state. When you are fully awake but still in bed trying to figure out how your day activity will be, you are automatically in the Alpha state. When these activities are being carried out - with lots of thinking and internal discussion - you are in either an Alpha state or in a low Gamma state.

If these state shifts are smooth, life feels less stressful, and our health and overall productivity will improve. Conversely, if these state shifts are rough, then our health will deteriorate. If we truly care about ourselves, we need to find ways to enhance the production of the beneficial chemicals while taking steps towards limiting the negative ones.

Activities that put us in A High Brainwave State, and Can also Damage Our Brain

Studies have shown that constant watching of television decreases our intelligence quotient (IQ) and creativity, and even leads to a certain amount of brain damage. Television has the ability to powerfully decrease brain functions, has a negative effect on academic achievement and makes even less use of your brain than when adding single digit numbers.

This is particularly dangerous when applied to children, as the following facts will show:

- Statistics show that TV viewing among kids is at a very high rate: Children from the age of 2-5 spend 32 hours a week in front of a TV - whether watching television, DVDs, DVRs, videos, or using a game console. Children between the age of 6-11 spend about 28 hours a week in front of the TV.
- About 71% of children between the age of 8-18 have a TV in their bedroom; 54% have a DVD/VCR player; 37% have cable/satellite TV; and 20% have premium channels.
- TV content can now be accessed more easily than ever before - on the Internet, via cell phones and iPods, etc. This has led to an increase in time spent viewing TV, even though TV set viewing has declined. About 41% of TV-viewing is now done online, via DVD or via a mobile platform.
- In about two-thirds of households, the TV is usually on during meals.
- In 53% of households, there are no rules about TV watching.
- In 51% of households, the TV is on most of the time.
- Kids with a TV in their bedroom spend an average of almost 1.5 hours more per day watching TV than kids without a TV in the bedroom.

The signs are clear - a lot of children are already addicted to TV from a young age. This is most likely caused by parents encouraging their toddlers and young children to watch television in order to have some leisure time for themselves.

How Does TV Damage our Brains?

Having seen how rampant TV watching is in this modern world, let us look at it side effects. Professor Herbert Krugman found that within 30 seconds of turning on the television, our brains become neurologically less able to make judgments about what we see and hear on the screen.

Surprised by how quickly the brain "shuts off", he went on to say that TV is a communication medium that effortlessly transmits huge quantities of information that the viewer did not think about at the time of exposure. The changes in brain function and thought process brought about by the medium of the screen alone allows the content of television to have a far greater impact on the mind.

What happens to the brain when watching TV is that the frontal lobe is effectively shut down. Our brain is the most sophisticated control system - responsible for organising, planning and sequencing behaviour for self-control, and moral judgment. However, our attention is completely subdued when watching TV. It reduces our ability to analyse critically what we are being told and what we are seeing; it makes us less motivated, less creative, makes us less perseverant in problem solving. There is also greater separation from thought and emotion, making human behaviour much more conformist. Not only does TV shut down a people's frontal lobes while they viewing, it also leads to underdeveloped frontal lobes after long-term use - where watching a lot of TV may even damage them as well.

It has been observed that some children and adults lash out and do things they shouldn't - a sign that their frontal lobes are underdeveloped. A study reported by The World Federation of Neurology shows that visual electronic media is affecting children by halting the process of frontal lobe development and affecting their ability to control potentially anti-social elements of their behaviour. The implications of this are very serious.

Children need to be allowed to be children; they should be encouraged to play outside with other children, interact and communicate with others as much as possible, rather than spending most of their time watching television. If more is done to thicken the fibres connecting the neurons in this part of their brains, the better the child's abilities will turn out to be.

Additionally, studies have shown that watching television induces low Alpha Waves in the human brain. Alpha Brainwaves - which are associated with relaxed meditative states as well as suggestibility - can be beneficial, where they promote relaxation and insight. However, too much time spent in the low Alpha State - which will happen with too much TV - can cause unfocussed daydreaming and an inability to concentrate. Researchers say that watching TV is similar to staring at a blank wall for several hours. If you are watching television, you are less conscious and less able to understand the reason you are being told or shown something.

Television Safe Exposure Guideline

Here is the Recommended Daily Allowance (RDA) for watching television:

- Children under three should see no screen entertainment.
- After this age, television viewing of good quality programmes should be limited to at most one hour a day.
- Teenagers should be limited to one-and-a-half hours per day of watching TV.
- For adults, the limit to watching TV should be two hours per day.

Bring Alpha - the best Brainwave - into Your Life

Have you ever asked yourself why babies sleep when you sing a soft lullaby? Or why a child moves his body when he hears the sound of music? Research into the impact of sounds and brain activity has yielded much evidence about the effects of music on mood and behaviour.

These findings, of course, are not a surprise to musicians, because the self-healing effects of music is known to every culture on earth. These observations show that music moves our brainwaves. Importantly, it offers the simplest path to an Alpha State, without demanding that you fall sleep in the process.

If we use music to alter our brainwaves, we can enhance our creativity or diminish stress. It is a simple formula: the faster the music, the faster the heart beats. Like slower breathing, a lower heartbeat creates less stress, and helps the body heal itself. Conversely, faster heartbeats create much stress, and may bring more danger to human health.

Different Types of Music that Shift Our Brainwaves

- Hip-Hop music has been found to get the nervous system stimulated to an excited state, and can sometimes stimulate one into exhibiting some very dynamic behaviour;
- Big bang music comforts us and engages our motion;
- Rock music is known to stir up passionate activities, and is one way to get rid of daily stress;
- Any form of South American movie can set our heart racing, get us moving, both relaxing us and awakening us at the same time;
- Jazz, Blues and Calypso are good at inspiring and uplifting. These forms of music help release deep joy and sadness that may be experienced at the time of listening.
- Classical music is good at helping gain more improved memory and concentration, especially when played in the background while learning.
- Studies have shown that slower Baroque pieces can help create a mentally-stimulating environment, to enhance creativity and innovative power.
- Romantic songs go a long way to help us increase our sense of love and sympathy.
- Hymns, gospels and all other religious music help us feel a deep peace and spiritual awareness, and are also good at helping one overcome all worries and pains.
- Impressionistic music can unlock dreamlike images that put one in touch with their own unconscious thoughts and belief systems.

- New Age music - which is also known as Ambient music - has been said to be quite effective in inducing of a state of relaxed alertness, which in turn helps one take control of stress levels.

Potential Electromagnetic Signals from Cellphones can Change Your Brainwaves and Behaviour

Have you ever asked yourself why some hospitals ban the use of cellphones in their premises? This is because the electromagnetic transmissions emanating from the phones can interfere with sensitive electrical devices - and our brain falls into this category because all our thoughts, sensations and actions arise from the bioelectricity generated by neurons, which are then transmitted through the complex circuit inside your skull.

The electrical signals between the neurons generate electric fields, which radiate out of the brain tissue as electrical waves. These waves can be picked up by using electrodes that touch a person's scalp. The measurement of such brainwaves in EEGs provide powerful insights into the brain's functions, which makes it a valuable diagnostic tool for doctors. Indeed, brainwaves are fundamental to the internal workings of the mind.

Brainwaves can be controlled by transcranial magnetic stimulation (TMS). This technique uses powerful pulses of electromagnetic radiation that are beamed into a person's brain, to jam or excite particular brain circuits. Although a cellphone is much less powerful than TMS, the question still remains: Could the electrical signals coming from a phone affect certain brainwaves operating in resonance with cell phone transmission frequencies? After all, the caller's cerebral cortex is just centimetres away from the radiation broadcast from the phone. Can it change with a healthy person's conscious and unconscious mental activity and state of arousal?

Rodney Croft - of the Brain Science Institute at Swinburne University of Technology in Melbourne, Australia - tested whether cell phone transmissions could alter a person's brainwaves, by monitoring the brainwaves of 120 healthy men and women with a Nokia 6110 cell phone strapped to their heads. A computer controlled the phone's transmissions in a double-blind experimental design. Croft found out that when the cellphone was transmitting, the power of the characteristic Alpha Brainwave pattern was boosted significantly, with the increased alpha wave activity greatest in brain tissue directly beneath the cell phone. This lends credence to observation that the phone was responsible for the observed effect.

Another set of findings was carried out by James Horne and his colleagues at the Loughborough University Sleep Research Centre in England, which not only showed that cellphone signals alter a person's behaviour during the call, but that the effects of the disrupted brain-wave patterns continued long after the phone had been switched off. This study was carried out using the Nokia 6310 model phones, which were attached to the head of 10 healthy but sleep-deprived men.

The researcher monitored the men's brainwaves by EEG, while the phone was switched on and off by a remote computer. The phones were also switched between "standby modes", "listen modes" and "talk modes" of operation for an interval of 30 minutes on different nights. The experiment revealed that after the phone was switched to talk mode, Delta Brainwave patterns remained dampened for nearly one hour after the phone was shut off, with the men remaining awake twice as long after the phone transmitting in talk mode was shut off.

Although these men had been deprived of sleep from the night before the test was carried out, they could not fall asleep for nearly one hour after the phone had been operating without their knowledge. This shows that cellphone transmissions can affect a person's brainwaves, resulting in persistent effects on their behaviour. Interestingly, Horne feels that cellphones are not damaging, because cellphone power is low, also taking into consideration the fact that everyone is surrounded by electromagnetic clusters radiating from all kinds of electronic devices in our modern world. Since electromagnetic radiation can have an effect on mental behaviour when transmitting at the proper frequency, it follows that cellphones cannot subsequently have an effect. However, cellphones in talk mode seem to be particularly well-tuned to frequencies that affect brainwave activity.

Croft emphasised that there are no health worries from these new findings. However, the exciting thing to note here is that it allows you to have a look at how you might modulate your brain functions, which tells us something about how the brain works on a fundamental level. Therefore, the importance of this work is in illuminating the fundamental workings of brain scientists, and in showing how they can learn a great deal about how brainwaves respond and what brainwaves do.

Brainwave Therapies

Life is all about rhythms. We are constantly subject to the rhythms of day and night, the change of the seasons, tension and relaxation, and the changing rhythms of our brainwaves. Each impulse inside or outside our bodies has to somehow be processed by our consciousness. As such, we can say that health and medical conditions correspond to changes in natural brain rhythms.

Cause and Effect of Wrong Rhythms

A change in our brain rhythm can change our wellbeing. Sometimes, the brain forgets to adapt to a natural change in rhythmic behaviour: depending on the situation, it tunes itself to rest, relax, concentrate or be tense. This happens when our inner rhythm no longer corresponds to the outer. The stress which we experience due to overwork, pressure, loss or unfinished business automatically increases our brain frequencies, forcing the brain to work in high gear at all times, which results in our brain losing its original rhythmic patterns.

Rhythms of Life

As we have mentioned earlier, our conscious and subconscious life take place mostly within four frequency ranges (if you accept that the Gamma State almost has the same characteristics as the Beta State):

- Wakefulness, Concentration, Alertness, Fear (Beta Rhythms, 14Hz-30Hz);
- Relaxation, State of Rest, Sleepiness (Alpha Rhythms, 7.5Hz-13.5 Hz);
- Light sleep/Deep meditation/Dreaming (Theta Rhythms, 4Hz- 7Hz, which supports memory, creativity and intuition); and
- Deep Sleep (Delta Rhythms 0.5Hz-3.5Hz, which supports regeneration, healthy immune system & all healing processes).

Holistic Induction Therapy

Holistic induction therapy programmes help the brain to mirror its own harmonious rhythms, reminding it of its original, correct oscillatory behaviour. The brain is carefully guided to oscillate back to its natural rhythms, and to change from one frequency range to another, in a manner appropriate to a given situation.

Contrary to the stimulation caused by different therapy methods, holistic induction is based on the introduction - through the medium of the skin - of vibrations innate to the brain. It does not force a change of the brain frequency, but makes an offer that the brain can decide to accept from moment to moment. The responsibility for that decision lies primarily with the part of the brain called the thalamus.

The thalamus monitors the impressions that are coming in from the outside - for instance, hearing, sight and sensation. Also known as the "gate to consciousness", the thalamus takes in the electrical impulses of the induction programme introduced through the skin. When it recognises these impulses as system-analogous ones which correspond to its own original rhythms, it will then catalyse the whole human organism to resonate and oscillate in the natural brainwave rhythms.

Not Treating the Brain

Medical studies shows that holistic induction therapy does not alter the characteristics of the brainwaves themselves - rather, they only affect the brain's rhythmical behaviour. Rest and relaxation are allowed to enter into the overworked and overstimulated areas of the brain, which means that potentially blocked symptoms can return to normalcy. Meanwhile, the symptoms of disease - which are connected to specific information blockages - are allowed to dissolve. As such, induction therapy is not so much a case of treating the brain, but rather creates a situation that treats the body like the brain.

About EEG Devices

Electroencephalography (EEG) is the recording of electrical activity along the scalp, by use of an electroencephalogram. EEG measures voltage fluctuations that result from ionic current flows within the neurons of the brain.

In clinical contexts, EEG refers to the recording of the brain's spontaneous electrical activity over a short period of time - usually from 20-40 minutes - as recorded using multiple electrodes which are placed on the patient's scalp. EEG is a valuable tool for research and diagnosis, and is used to diagnose sleep disorders, coma, encephalopathy, and brain death.

Derivatives of the EEG technique include evoked potentials (EP), which involves averaging the EEG activity that is time-locked to the presentation of a stimulus of some sort (visual, somatosensory, or auditory). Event-related potentials (ERPs) refer to average EEG responses that are time-locked to more complex processing of stimuli. The latter technique is used in cognitive science, cognitive psychology, and psycho physiological research.

How Brainwaves Affect Our Behaviour

Studies have shown that learning whilst in the Alpha State enhances the performance of the student. It also helps the student to develop interest in studies more than they would have ever learned while in other high-frequency brainwaves.

It has been noted that induced Alpha Waves enable the student to assimilate more information, with greater long-term retention. The brainwave indicates a relaxed state of mind, good for inspiration and the ability to learn fast. There is more understanding of the role of Theta Brainwaves in behavioural learning, because this state indicates a high state of mental concentration. The presence of Theta Brainwaves has been associated with increased receptivity for learning and decreased filtering by the left hemisphere.

How Brainwaves Affect Our Work and Relationships

Brainwaves play very vital roles in our work, relationships and every other aspect of our lives. Listening to brainwave music acts as a form of meditation, which has been found to help prepare the human brain for daily work, reduce the risk of illnesses, decrease stress levels and keep one in the right frame of mind at all times.

These brainwaves effects go a long way towards increasing our productivity at work, and towards helping our relationships to work better. With increased concentration and calmness, we are able to handle situations more calmly and peacefully.

Chapter Four

The Left and Right of It

I have been described as the sort of person that thrives on chaos. I work mostly on emotion and intuition, and I'm also very creative and have a very out-going personality. However, when it comes to setting definite goals and working towards them, I'm quite hopeless.

My significant other, my son, on the other hand, approaches every situation with logic, hard work and dedication. He prefers to analyse a thousand different factors in order to reach a logical decision. It takes time, but it seems to work for him. Occasionally, our different natures and approaches lead to spats - but mostly they allow us to complement one another. Still, sometimes, I wonder why we are so different; we have similar upbringings, a similar education, and have chosen to work in the same field. Yet these differences are there and they are glaringly obvious.

Have you ever wondered why some people prize logic and order above all, yet others are guided solely by their emotions? Well, the answer lies in our brains - specifically, in the two hemispheres of the brain. The human brain - or rather, the cerebrum - is divided into two distinct parts - the left and the right, each hemisphere with its own set of responsibilities and functions.

It is almost like they have their own domains, over which each part of the brain reigns. They not only process information differently, but also provide us with outputs of this processed information in different ways. Together, these halves are known as the left-right brain, although the correct term for them would be left and right "hemispheres".

Physically, both these hemispheres appear similar to each other. However, anatomically speaking, they are remarkably different. Our physiology is wired such that the left-brain controls the right part of the body, while the right-brain controls the left part. For instance, when we see something from our left eye, the image is processed in the right part of the brain. If the right part of the brain is damaged for some reason, the left part of our body will be affected.

The understanding of the two hemispheres and how they perform was first studied in the 1960s. American psychologist and biologist Roger W. Sperry began his research in this field, and he discovered that a single human brain has very distinct ways of thinking, processing information, and functioning.

The right side of the brain, he discovered, had the potential to look at things holistically. The right side would consider the big picture, and process information in its entirety. The left side of the brain, on the other hand, broke information into tiny units, and analysed each of these units separately. It then pieced the information together to obtain a more logical and sequential understanding.

In the years to come, further research proved Sperry's work to be right and ground breaking, and he was awarded the Nobel Prize in 1981 for his significant contribution. Before Sperry's research, the brain was considered to be a single, homogenous organ that simply functioned differently in different people - and it was only after Sperry that the medical and sciences communities realised that the actual workings of these two distinct hemispheres of the brain were different.

The Why of It: Left Brain-Right Brain Functions

The left side of the brain is considered to be the logical half, and is responsible for all analytical and logical thoughts - in other words, the left hemisphere operates sequential and logical parameters, and is responsible for rational thought and behaviour. The focus is also on verbal and logical processing of information. Our speech originates in the left side of the brain, as it is this side that learns language, thinks, and speaks.

The right side of the brain has a completely different set of responsibilities. It is more visual and spatial based, and processes information almost simultaneously. As soon as you have a visual cue, the right-brain begins to work. The right-brain is often called the "holistic side", because it is non-linear and has a certain intuitive aspect to it. It looks at the whole picture before it begins to focus on the minute details. It is often believed that the right hemisphere of the brain is the more creative one, owing to its spatial and visual inclinations, whereas the left-brain is what makes us rational and decisive.

Owing to its analytical and sequential processing nature, the left-brain is often called the "digital" side of the brain. This is the part that controls calculations, reading, writing, and logical thought. The right-brain has control over creative thoughts, and is often called the "analog" brain. It is this part of the brain that has all the three dimensional senses. It controls creativity, and has an inclination towards the finer things and senses.

It is believed that some people are more right-brain oriented, while others are dominated by the left hemisphere of the brain. Notice how people have different reactions to the same situation? It is usually because there is a difference in the way their brains process information, coming up with alternative solutions to different problems. However, there is no "right" or "wrong" here; this is simply how the body works, and this is what makes each one of us different.

Some people are aware of their natural preferences, and understand which part of the brain is more dominant for them. If you know what your natural inclinations are, you can consciously learn to activate and hone the other less dominant part of your brain.

By activating both hemispheres of the brain and channelling their power naturally, people can become more proficient in anything they desire. They are able to take in the bigger picture, as well as concentrate on the smaller details. They are also able to retain more knowledge. Children who have been subjected to experiments that activate both sides of their brains have been observed to be more proficient in their studies, and have a keener instinct for mathematics. I myself have experienced this. When I realised that I was more right-brain oriented, and was making my decisions more intuitively than logically, I decided to change the situation.

There are some simple exercises you can engage in to activate both your brain hemispheres. Learning logical sequencing and applying logical thought using visual cues can help make the left-right brain connection even stronger, so that you are able to channel the power of your entire brain.

In addition, it is often believed that a person's handedness is an indication of which side of the brain is more dominant. This is not true. Although some functions of our brain are lateralised, scientists believe that this is only a tendency.

Scientists are studying the structural and chemical variances between different brain functions and the two hemispheres. They are comparing this data with the chemical variances between functions in the same hemisphere, as well as between functions in two different sets of brains. One thing is clear - unless a person has undergone the removal of a cerebral hemisphere, no person is only left-brained or right-brained. It is only when these two hemispheres work together in harmony that a human can function normally - and although one part of the brain may be slightly more dominant than the other, the two work together to sustain human life.

Right-Left Characteristics: Which One Are You?

The left- and right-brain are very similar to each other physically. However, there are some anatomical differences that lend these hemispheres their general characteristics.

In right-handed individuals, the language functions - especially grammar and vocabulary - typically originate in the left hemisphere. This has been found to be true in at least 90% of right-handed subjects in a research. In the same research, it was found that almost 50% of left-handed people also had their language and vocabulary functions originating from the left-brain hemisphere.

Some language functions are in the right-brain hemisphere as well. Prosodic language, for instance, is located in the right-brain. Other nuances of language - such as intonation and accents - are also located in the right-brain.

Research has shown that in about 95% of right-handed men - and more than 90% of right-handed women - certain aspects of speech processing, language, and vocabulary are dominant through the left-brain. The incidence of the left-brain's superiority in language is lower in left-handed people. In a group of left-handed people, about 75% of men and 61% of women showed left-brain superiority in language.

With the help of modern neuroimaging methods and magnetic resonance imaging, it has been found that both hemispheres are involved in many aspects of speech and language development, processing and function, though the imaging studies also concluded that there is a dominance of one part of the brain over another. The left part would be activated more when language is being formulated. Therefore, it is wrong to assume that language or math - or any other function - is localised in any one hemisphere of the brain, and it is also wrong to assume that the other hemisphere has nothing to do with it.

Some of the other visual and auditory processes - which are often associated with the right brain in popular psychology - lie in both the brain hemispheres, even though the right hemisphere does show some superiority in this regard. Spatial manipulation, creativity and artistic abilities, and facial perception are some of the popularly believed right-brain processes which actually lie in both the hemispheres.

The brain also has the bilateral parietal regions, which contain some of the analytical and logical functions of the brain. It is here that the numerical estimations, mental calculations, and comparisons lie. The left side of the parietal region is associated with retrieval of facts, and with making exact calculations. Scientists believe that this could be due to the fact that these processes are related to linguistic processing, which occurs in the left side of the brain.

It is important to understand that there are different kinds of skills within a parent skill. For instance, within math, there are a lot of different skills, starting from the ability to estimate the number of items into two sets of things to making detailed calculations. This processing of math takes place in both the hemispheres - only, each hemisphere is responsible for a very specific type of skill.

Damage to either of the hemispheres can cause difficulty in processing math. For tasks such as counting and multiplication tables, the left hemisphere is predominant, because these tasks rely on memory. Visual estimation - such as estimating number of objects in a set - usually belongs to the right hemisphere.

Both the hemispheres have their own set of cognitive abilities; therefore, both contribute to being logical and creative. It is almost impossible to categorise functions and limit them to only one side of the brain.

For example, a person may not be able to produce speech if there is damage to the left part of the brain. Similar damage to the right half of the brain may not produce similar problems in speech - but this is not an indication of the right hemisphere's nonparticipation in the speech function. Damage to the right brain may cause some other kind of serious damage to language. So, even though the left hemisphere does have a larger contribution in producing language, the right hemisphere is involved in it too - and the ability to speak the way we do normally comes from the collaboration of the two hemispheres.

Both the left and right brains have their own inherent strengths and weaknesses. The normal functioning of the human body requires these two hemispheres to be working, both together and separately. If a person is dominated by either the left-brain or the right-brain, they will demonstrate a specific type of behaviour. Here is a table that illustrates the varying characteristics of left- and right-dominant individuals:

Left-Side Dominant People	Right-Side Dominant People
• Make logical arguments; • Tend to have an answer to most questions; • Are oriented towards their future; • Usually keep very busy; • Do not have much body awareness; • Tend to ignore any symptoms of physical ailments; • Have a tendency to be nervous and restless; • Learn quickly, especially under direction; • Have a tendency to develop hypochondria; • Have inner visions and deep feelings, but would not know what to do with them; • Usually like to take dominant, leadership type roles, and vie for high positions in their profession; • Are task oriented; • Need success and recognition to be happy; • Thrive on order and structure;	• Have a tendency to talk about negative feelings; • Are oriented towards the past; • Try out several therapies, but do not persist; • Tend to be dissatisfied, moody and emotionally unstable; • Tend to be pessimistic, and often border on being self-destructive; • Are slow to improve any physical or emotional conditions; • Are charismatic, extroverted and very popular; • Tend to be creative and interested in creative activities, like art, music, and literature; • Tend to need a lot of space; • Work on many activities simultaneously; • Are very communicative and inventive; • Tend to be spiritually inclined; • Are easily inspired by others; • Are incapable of separating ideas from feelings;

• Develop very rigid views about their own goals and identity; • Demonstrate a problem-solving approach; • Prefer logical sequencing and reasoning in everything; and • Are easy to hypnotise.	• Have little self-control; • Are under constant stress; • Tend to be obese; • Tend to be fatalistic, especially when they have chronic diseases or life-threatening diseases; and • Solve problems intuitively

As I have mentioned earlier, I'm more right-brain oriented, which means that I lean towards the past and need a lot of space for my creative processes. I tend to rely more on my feelings and intuitions when solving problems. I also get inspired easily and often and am deeply spiritual. In addition to this, I am very communicative, and my friends and family find my company extremely enjoyable. In fact, I am considered rather charismatic.

However, I am also constantly wavering in my thoughts, and this leads to a lot of stress. I procrastinate, and I am not particularly inclined towards improving my health, which is also often a cause for concern. These are classic characteristics of right brain dominance, and thus, another indication of my right brain preference.

Out of Sync: Left-Right Imbalance

There is a very close connection between the left and right hemispheres. If one side is impaired, it may cause problems with the functions on the other side. This is because the functioning of the two hemispheres is not independent. For instance, if the left temporal-parietal junction is damaged, it causes a neurological condition known as dyscalculia, where a person is unable to manipulate numbers and has poor arithmetic skills. This condition may trigger hyperactivity in the right hemisphere of the brain, triggering conditions like depression.

Depression is essentially a right hemisphere condition, in which there is increased processing of pessimistic thoughts, negative emotions, and unconstructive reflection and thinking. When the right-brain is thus hyperactive in processing pessimistic thoughts, the left-brain becomes hypoactive - and the important processing of arousal, vigilance, introspection and self-reflection does not occur properly, thus fuelling the depression.

Moreover, when the right hemisphere is not performing its duties well, the left hemisphere steps in, and becomes more involved in processing any pleasurable experiences. This is generally a right-brain function, so the left-brain is unable to do it well. Ultimately, it becomes less involved in the decision-making processes and logical sequencing which are primarily its domain - causing a decrease in the person's decision-making and rational abilities.

Any imbalance between the two hemispheres of the brain has a direct impact on the person's abilities to function normally. Left-brain lesions or damage usually results in omissive responses and errors, whereas right-brain lesions can lead to commissive responses. This means that lesions on the left side of the brain will hurt your memory, and you may forget to do certain things, while the lesions on the right side of the brain may make you commit actions that you may not have any control over. Amnesia is usually a left-brain condition, while delusional misidentification syndromes and Capgras delusion are usually caused due to lesions or damage on the right side of the brain.

Although I have never experienced a very stark imbalance between the two hemispheres of my brain, I strongly felt that I should bring more balance, because I did tend to be slightly negative and depressed. For those who suffer from brain injuries or any other condition that has caused lesions in their brain, it is important to get medical aid immediately, so that the problems can be corrected before it becomes difficult to manage.

Though the left- and right-sides of the brain are usually seen as having different functions, the two hemispheres are tied to each other through a very complex connection. A balance between the two hemispheres is very important to maintain a person's cognitive functioning and balance. Any imbalance between the two results in extreme personalities, and may lead to neurotic conditions such as depression.

Fortunately, scientific research has been able to discover certain exercises and activities that can help produce a more balanced development of both hemispheres, so that you can have greater left-right brain balance. A glaring example of this is the teaching of mathematics using the abacus. The use of an abacus at a very early age can help children develop their math, visual, and spatial skills. This simultaneously helps in the development of both the left hemisphere and the right hemisphere of the brain.

Chapter Five

Super Foods for Smarter Brains

What Connects the Brain to the Tummy?

Almost every parent can relate to that moment when they suddenly realise how developed their 15-year-olds look; the pair of jeans you got them last week is falling a few inches shorter, and even the T-shirt seems to have shrunk during the laundry. Is it just the clothes, or have they really grown?

Proud parents would vouch that it felt like only yesterday when their little ones were holding on to their fingers and learning to walk - whereas now, they are standing shoulder-to-shoulder and are rearing to take on the world.

However, being the tallest in the class doesn't always translate into being the top of the lot. "Big" and "fat" are words that more often form the adjectives before that most infamous term: "Bully". The idea is simple: faster growth doesn't necessarily bring along with it smarter brains.

Eating habits have long been associated with the development of our body, especially that of the brain. No doubt that food is the fuel that keeps your body running - but the nutrient value of that food determines whether you are growing in size or developing a strong body.

How Food Impacts the Development of the Brain

Our body needs energy to function effectively. The heart, the kidneys, and the brain - all need a steady supply of energy. The body is growing every second, where millions upon millions of cells are busy multiplying, growing and developing into a healthy human being - without our actual knowledge or awareness. This development begins much earlier, even before we are born, when the major parts of our body develop into organs during the prenatal stage itself.

However, unlike the other organs of the body, the brain has a multitude of functions to attend to. The primary function of the heart is to pump blood, while the brain needs to perform a plethora of things, including taking care of all your actions, thoughts and even mood changes.

What is Our Brain, and How does it Work?

Like your body, nearly 80 percent of the brain is also water. An adult brain weighs around 1.5kg, and is made up of millions and millions of nerve cells. These are the main functionary cells - neurons - that are responsible for receiving and sending messages to various parts of the body. Every voluntary action you make is related to the brain, as it is these numerous neurons that give the command for the action depending on the situation.

The mass of neuron cells is held together by glial cells, which also nourish these nerve cells. There is a tiny space between neurons called the synapse, through which signals are passed between the neurons, through the release of chemicals called neurotransmitters.

To perform all of these functions, the brain takes up about 25 percent of your daily calorie intake. However, food not only gives brain the energy to function effectively, it also forms the brain cells and membranes. It is fat that forms the neuronal membranes, as well as the protective layer around the neurons (called the myelin sheath).

Proteins too play a role in sending signals between neurons. Remember the chemical neurotransmitter that is released while sending signals? Well, the building blocks of protein - amino acids - mostly form the neurotransmitter - so, if you need faster communication between neurons, you sure need to ensure that you get enough proteins and fats. Thus - speaking both chemically and physiologically - our food habits have an impact on our brain's structure and functioning.

When there is a lack of food or required nutrients, your brain is unable to function to its full capacity, leading to lack of concentration, focus, or even in delay for responding to situations or reaching logical conclusions.

What are the Best Brain Foods?

Whatever you consume is food - whether fizzy soft drinks, a hot espresso, a packet of potato chips, or a plateful of rice, vegetables and steak - and all these foods have an impact on your brain depending on what you have, how much and for how long.

There are more than enough everyday examples to explain this concept - and the tea that totally wakes you up in the morning and puts your mind on full alert would probably the best of example of them all. However, not all categories of food have this instant effect on the brain, and different foods will affect different functions of the brain.

Now that we know that food choices can influence the way our brain develops, let's check out what are the types of food that we need to feed our brain. Broadly speaking, your brain needs three basic nutrients: carbohydrates, proteins and fats. Any diet that ensures a balanced blend of these nutrients will do loads of good for your brain.

So far, we have been discussing the importance of energy supply to the brain. The fuel for your brain functions comes from the carbohydrates that you consume. The glucose released during the burning of calories is the fuel that keeps your brain running.

The digestive system breaks down the carbohydrates in food into glucose, which is then transported by the blood to various cells for energy. There are two types of carbohydrates: simple and complex.

Simple carbs are the ones found in your daily bread, biscuits, cookies, and jam, and can be easily broken down into glucose. Weight watchers are generally advised to avoid anything "white" - e.g., refined or polished rice, white bread, potatoes, etc. - as they all contain simple carbs. This is because these provide a lot of calories that will be released a too fast a rate. When there is an excess of this type of energy produced in the body, it gets converted into fat, which is stored for future use.

Complex carbs come in the form of whole grain cereals, rice, and even vegetables. Although complex, they are good because it takes longer to break down these carbs into glucose - hence, they ensure a steady supply of energy. While choosing carbs, you will also need to check for the Glycemic Index (GI), which is the rate at which food is broken down into glucose and enters the blood. You should remember to avoid or lessen the intake of foods with a high GI.

Fats are the next set of nutrients that are essential for the functioning of the brain. Many vitamins need fat in order to dissolve, for it is only then that they can be absorbed into the body.

Similar to carbohydrates, fats can be classified into good ("poly-saturated" fat and "unsaturated" fat) and bad ("saturated" fat and "trans" fat). When deciding on a diet, you will need to get your facts right about fat.

The good fats are mostly the ones available in plant oils or plant-based oils (like seeds) and in Omega-3 fatty acids which are found in seafood. These are good for the body, as they lower the blood's cholesterol level, and decrease the risk of ailments, compared to saturated fat and trans fat.

Powerful proteins protect your neurons from degenerating diseases. As mentioned earlier, they are also the building blocks of the neurotransmitters - so a protein-rich diet - which will include pulses, beans, fish, meat and dairy products - is essential for the proper functioning of the brain.

Top 10 Brain Foods that Boost Brain Power and Memory

Have you ever wondered why you take longer to tackle a math problem, or why you are a couple of seconds slower in reaching a logical conclusion, compared to your peers? You probably would have blamed your genes or poor schooling for it. But while these factors do play a role in determining your IQ, it also does depend on your diet. Yes, you read that right - you can also eat your way to cleverness!

1.	**Nothing Fishy Here** Studies have shown that students who eat seafood - such as salmon or tuna - on a regular basis have a better IQ than students who don't. This is because of the high content of Omega-3 fatty acids in them. These poly-saturated fats have been associated with greater focus and better academic performance in children. How does that happen? Omega-3 fatty acids aid in a faster transfer of signals from one neuron to another, which has an impact on the neurotransmitter pathways in the brain. The faster the signals move, the quicker the brain can make decisions and give commands to execute them. Omega-3 fatty acids are known to increase blood flow, thereby ensuring a better supply of energy to the brain cells. The body cannot generate these good fats - so, you will need to have a diet rich in them by adding seafood - such as tuna, mackerel and salmon - to your eating habits. You should consume three to four servings of the seafood for desired results. Does that alarm vegetarians and vegans? Not to worry: there are many plants that are sources of Omega-3 fatty acids, including flaxseeds, walnuts, and soybeans. If you are not too keen on having seafood that often, you could also munch on a handful of walnuts every day for smart brains.

2.	**Wholesome Whole Grains** Whole grain is the latest buzzword amongst fitness freaks. Whether it is whole grain wheat, breads or cereals, the clamour for it just seems to be getting louder. What do these wonderful grains offer your brain? Firstly, these complex carbs ensure that there is a steady supply of oxygen to the brain. Opting for whole grain products more regularly would also reduce the risk of heart ailments, while ensuring better blood flow that helps keep your brain alert. Whole grains are also great sources of Vitamin B, which helps in boosting your memory power. Opt for at least one whole grain item or meal every day.
3.	**Egging on Meat** As the powerhouses of proteins, eggs are imperative for the development of brain. The chemical known as tryptophan - which is found in eggs - helps the brain to manufacture a neurotransmitter known as serotonin. Seratonin, which is also known as the "good mood" chemical, helps in combating anxiety, and makes you feel content and relaxed. It would help lift the mood of children, and help them concentrate on their academic work. Eggs also provide you with the essential building blocks of the brain, known as choline. Choline is known to aid people in retaining their memory, and is a magic nutrient that can also slow down the aging process of the brain - ensuring that you will retain a strong memory, even in at a ripe old age. Whether served sunny side-up or boiled, eggs are perfect starters for any day. Even chicken, fish and kidney beans are known to possess choline, which belongs to the Vitamin B family. Ensure that you have two or three servings of lean meat every week for that perfect memory.

4.	**Go Green** Nature lovers have long been shouting out for a greener tomorrow. While a green cover is mandatory for life to continue peacefully on Earth, greens are must-haves on your dinner plate too. Fibre-rich carbs, such as broccoli, possess large quantities of Vitamin K, which helps in the release of serotonin. Veggies such as spinach and Brussels sprouts enhance cognitive ability, and help improve brainpower. Throw more veggies on to your salad plate to enjoy the benefits.
5.	**An Iota of Iodine** This mineral helps the thyroid gland produce growth hormones, which in turn are necessary for the development of the brain. This mineral, although essential, is only needed in very small amounts. It cannot be produced in the body - which means that you need to ensure that your body gets the right dose at regular intervals. The easiest and most common way of ensuring an adequate intake of iodine is by using iodised salt in your cooking.
6.	**Beckon the Berries** Berries contain folic acid and foliate, which helps in developing the brain of unborn babies, while also helping to prevent defects in them. Strawberries can act as great memory boosters, whilst blueberries are known to improve both the learning ability of the brain as well as motor skills. A handful of berries a day can be the best pal for your brain. Because you have a wide variety of these super berries to choose from, you will be able to avoid monotony, which may arise due to repetitive taste.

7.	**Fruitful Avocados** A fatty fruit, avocados are rich in Vitamin E, which increases blood flow. Good blood flow means that more oxygen gets to the brain, making it a healthier brain. Consequently, high blood pressure can wreck havoc with the functioning of brain. Avocados help in lowering blood pressure, which means it promotes better brain health. Other fruits known to boost memory include pomegranates and bananas, which are great sources of anti-oxidants, and help keep you focused.
8.	**Nutty Power** Among the users of the English language, the word "nutty" is generally meant to indicate a crazy idea or person. I still wonder how that came into being, as nuts are some of the best kinds of snacks that you can have for better brain health. The vitamin E founds in nuts helps promote better cognitive abilities in people, and they also help prevent the decline of cognitive functions during old age. Walnuts, almonds, cashews, pistachios - all offer the brain a handful of benefits, and may even prevent Alzheimer's Disease from occurring.
9.	**Beverages for the Brain** It's not just you who can enjoy a hot cup, but your brain as well, be it coffee, espresso, green tea or any other such beverage. A cup of coffee is the best way to pull you out of the bed, and it puts you in "alert mode" for the day. Caffeine blocks the chemicals that cause drowsiness, which means it helps keep the nerve cells in your brain active. If you are not into coffee, you can also try out green tea, which fights mental fatigue and allows you to concentrate better. A great anti-oxidant, green tea also improves your memory power. However, despite these benefits, drink them in moderation: one or two cups every day.

10.	**Dark Chocolate**
	We saved the best for the last. Who can resist a bar of dark chocolate? Old or young, all are fond of this dark delight - which is great, because this bar of happiness can keep your mind alert and focused. Eating chocolates ensures high levels of the neurotransmitter known as dopamine, which keeps you enthusiastic and happy. It has been found that having low levels of this "happy messenger" could lead to irritation and boredom. However, as with coffee and tea, you have to be careful not to overeat chocolates. Stick to one bar of dark chocolate every alternate day, and you will find a difference in your IQ levels.

Supplements for Super Brains

It is always advisable to obtain nutrients naturally, i.e., through food. Nothing beats the goodness of nutrients that you avail through food itself, as opposed to relying on supplementary capsules. However, in case your everyday diet fails to provide you with the required nutrients, you are left with no choice but to depend on health supplements. A common reason why people do not get the required nutrients from their diet is because most of these nutrients may get lost during cooking or processing.

Fish oil supplements are the most commonly recommended supplements for brainpower. The Omega-3 fatty acids in them are known to enhance memory power, and are important for keeping your cognitive abilities active. Among the vitamins, B and E are the most essential supplements needed to boost memory power.

Folic acid, another type of Vitamin B, is also highly recommended, as it improves memory, and helps you to stay focused. Vitamin B6 triggers the release of serotonin and dopamine.

However, you need to be sure and check with your doctor before starting use of any supplementary capsules. The wrong supplements or a high dosage of certain medicines may have very harmful side-effects.

Antioxidants in Brain Development?

You may have laughed when your grandfather was looking for his pair of reading glasses - when they are right on top of his nose. Have you ever paused to wonder why he would have so much trouble remembering what is literally right before his eyes? He probably forgot that he had already put on the glasses - which is a sign that memory, like other cognitive abilities, begin to decline as a person reaches old age.

Your body is constantly under the threat of oxidation, or the damaging action of oxygen. This normal wear and tear is a part of the aging process, which is why your memory fails when you age, and why you are unable to remember even the simplest of things.

Antioxidants protect your brain from this "wear and tear". You need to include more fruits and vegetables with high levels of antioxidants in them. In that respect, berries are considered the best for boosting your memory, due to their high levels of antioxidants.

All berries - blackberries, strawberries, and gooseberries - are great sources of antioxidants to enhance your immunity. The types of antioxidants in them include Vitamin C, Vitamin E, and flavonoids, which help form the much-needed arsenal for your body to guard against oxidation.

Have you ever envied those old folks who can still remember every single detail about their partners, loving them with a fervour that you can only wish for? Well, they probably took their diet seriously during the growing years, which ensured that they had the right quantity of nutrients regularly. Basically, while some foods help your to brain develop, the ones with antioxidants prevent your brain from decaying, thus keeping it active and alert - even in old age.

Dos and Don'ts for Brain Foods

The world in the 21st Century is seeing a weird problem. Those who have access to food have them in excess, but are still unable to make wise decisions when choosing their diet. On the contrary, we have the not-so-lucky ones who have to make do with whatever scraps of food that comes their way - who give no thought whatsoever about health or hygiene. The situation seems to be a grim, one with both the privileged and the poor having the wrong food items on their plates.

Let us start from the beginning: break your night fast at the earliest possible moment. Beginning the day with a hearty breakfast will ensure an alert mind. A drooping head during class in all likelihood indicates that a child has had either a poor breakfast, or none at all. A steaming cup of tea in the morning would make both your brain and mind alert for the day ahead. The bottom line is, a late night party should never be made as an excuse for a late breakfast. Also, it is important to eat three regular meals every day. This would ensure a steady supply of energy to the brain, which will keep it active.

Once you get your food timetable in order, then you should classify food into the good and the bad. You need to steer clear of the bad that falls into the category known as "junk". Junk food takes up all your appetite while simultaneously contributing very less in terms of nutrients to your body. French fries and pastries are all loaded with trans fat, which is harmful to the body.

Additionally, all the fat you take on while munching the yummy-yet-unhealthy stuff might even make you depressed. Emotional eating - especially due to depression - would further affect the development of the brain - and the effects are especially dangerous during a person's growing years.

Even in the good foods category, you need to be aware of how you should be eating. Nuts are great sources of good health - but only when eaten unroasted and unsalted. Adding too much salt or deep-frying them would relegate them to the junk food category. The extra salt and oil would disrupt the cholesterol and sodium levels of the body, and wreak havoc on your system.

The flip side of having anything good is that too much of it will have a negative impact. While coffee is a great stimulant, too much caffeine can trigger nervousness. It causes the release of adrenaline, which is generally released as a response to stressful situations. As such, you may become more anxious, and lose the ability to think or focus clearly.

You should opt for foods with a low Glycemic Index (GI), as these would release glucose slowly to the body. As mentioned earlier, GI affects the body's "moods".

Another "don't" alert is specifically for mothers-to-be. Binging on junk foods during pregnancy can lead to lower IQ levels among the offspring, according to the experts. Unhealthy eating patterns during the prenatal period may affect the maturing brain of the foetus, and may eventually lead to decreased cognitive functions for the child in the later stages.

Eat and eat well for the best results in your exams. They really meant it when they came up with the term "food for thought"!

Finally, drink plenty of water every day. How much water do we need to drink has been an endless debate - but one thing is clear, the figure varies from person to person. The rule of thumb, then, is to drink enough water to keep your brain from getting dehydrated.

The Balancing Act

"What happens when two people talk? That is really the basic question here, because that's the basic context in which all persuasion takes place."

- Malcolm Gladwell (Author, The Tipping Point)

Did you know that the electromagnetic signal produced by your heart is registered in the brainwaves of people around you?

When you exude the energy of positive emotions such as joy, serenity and enthusiasm in the presence of a friend, (s)he will pick up your emotional vibes - and shortly after, their own emotional and mental states will be "entrained" - that is, "pulled along" - with yours.

Our emotions are a form of energy - and since different emotions are simply different vibrations of energy, emotions can entrain each other. That's how our emotions influence each other, why your feelings change from moment to moment, depending on the people or the environment around you.

With a well-exercised brain, you can easily pick up emotions from people around you - and you will have a choice on how to react to it. Imagine an overstressed brain with overly high Beta Brainwaves: How will such a person behave? I can imagine them being stressed, angry, frustrated, and tense.

In my coaching practice, having a powerful brain has to coexist with a beautiful heart. I started realising the effect when my sons came up to me and asked: "Dad, what's wrong with you?" I always pause for six seconds, and reflect on what's happening - a practice that I developed over the years, to feel what's inside of me before replying to his question; that's the conversation with the brain systems.

When you understand something about how the brain moves from resistance to buy-in, you'll have a huge edge - because no matter what your message is, you need to talk to the brain. I have always been curious about how I talk to my brain which has an impact on my emotions, or vice versa. If I have difficulties in the conversation with my brain, what will potentially happen if I need to get a "buy-in"?

Mark Goulston came up with three crucial concepts that can empower you to see what's happening behind another person's eyes:

1.	**The Three-Part Brain** This is split into: • **The Lower Reptilian Brain:** The "fight-or-flight" part of your brain. This region of your brain is all about acting and reacting, without a lot of thinking going on. It can leave you frozen in a perceived crisis - the "deer-in-the-headlights" response. • **The Middle Mammal Brain:** This is the seat of your emotions (Call it your inner drama queen). It's where powerful feelings - love, joy, sadness, anger, grief, jealousy, pleasure - arise. • **The Upper or Primate Brain:** This is the part that weighs a situation logically and rationally, and generates a conscious plan of action. This brain collects data from the reptile and mammal brains, sifts it, analyses it, and makes practical, smart, and ethical decisions. All of these parts have power over how you think and act every day. To a small extent, these three brains work together. To a greater extent, however, they tend to pull apart and function independently - especially when we're under stress. When that happens and the reptile or mammal brain takes control, the human thinking brain is eclipsed, and we shift into primal brain functions.
2.	**The Amygdala Hijack (or The Death of the Rational)** This is a term that was first coined by psychologist Daniel Goleman, the originator of the concept of emotional intelligence. The term "hijack" is appropriate, because at that point, your brain's intelligent and sensible pilot - the frontal cortex- is no longer in control. Instead, the snake is flying the plane.

Goleman, no doubt, was keen on this concept - because when you undergo an amygdala hijack, your emotional intelligence goes out the window. It is used to describe a situation in which a person responds based on emotional rather than intellectual factors. Importantly, the emotional response is often inappropriate. The amygdala is the emotional centre of the human brain, which creates immediate responses when a person experiences fear or threats, overriding the neuro cortex or intellect.

Here are some strategies that can be invoked to avoid an amygdala hijack:

- **Be in the Moment!** Apply the six-second rule. Think physiology. Those amygdala hijacking chemicals in your brain require approximately six seconds to dissipate. Use this knowledge to your advantage by redirecting your emotions for those critical six seconds - refocus your thoughts towards a positive emotion. Try counting six breaths until the reaction to lose control subsides. Leverage on humour or empathy to neutralise the discussion. If you get along with this person in general, retain that relationship by evoking other emotions. Assess the situation; be cognizant of the other person's emotions; understand that everyone makes mistakes.
- **Be Reflective!** So the hijack happened - what next? Conduct a self-review of what happened. Once you identify the trigger(s), store this knowledge for future application. If the cortex is not involved, the amygdala operates on past information. Experience is the best teacher - so being mindful enables you to retrieve and apply this knowledge in the moment.
- Be **Proactive**! Think each encounter through, and anticipate possible stimuli. Keeping your cortex involved in the interaction process often help prevent the amygdala from completely taking over.

3.	**Mirror Neurons**
	Years ago, scientists studying specific nerve cells in the prefrontal cortices of macaque monkeys found that the cells fired when the monkeys threw a ball or ate a banana. Surprisingly, these same cells fired when the monkeys watched other monkeys perform these acts. Essentially, when Monkey #1 watched Monkey #2 toss a ball, the brain of the first monkey reacted just as if it had tossed the ball itself. Scientists initially nicknamed these cells "monkey see, monkey do" neurons. Later, they changed the name to mirror neurons, because these cells allow monkeys to mirror another being's actions in their own minds. The new name is more accurate - because we are finding that humans, just like macaques, have neurons that act as mirrors. In fact, studies suggest that these remarkable cells may form the basis for human empathy. That's because, in effect, they transport us into another person's mind, briefly making us feel what the person is feeling. In a 2007 article titled "*The Neurology of Self-Awareness*" in *Edge*, V. S. Ramachandran - a pioneer in mirror neuron research - commented: "Mark Goulston called these 'empathy neurons', or 'Dalai Lama neurons', for they are dissolving the barrier between self and others." In short, these cells may prove to be one way in which nature causes us to care about other people. However, new questions emerge when we look at mirror neurons from another angle: • Why is it that we often tear up when someone is kind to us? • Why is it that we get a warm feeling when someone understands us? • Why is it that a simple "Are you okay?" can so move us?

	The theory - which Goulston's clinical findings support - is that we constantly mirror the world, conforming to its needs, trying to win its love and approval. Each time we mirror the world, it creates a little reciprocal hunger to be mirrored back. If that hunger isn't filled, we develop what he refers to as "mirror neuron receptor deficit".

If you understand all the above, you'll know all you need to know about the brain science behind how you can reach out to anyone.

Chapter Six
The Balancing Act

Realising Emotional Types

World-renowned emotional intelligence expert Daniel Goleman has said: "The human brain hasn't had a hardware upgrade in about 100,000 years." - and according to him, most of us are still acting out of the ancient "fight-or-flight" response. An upgrade is long overdue.

Goleman battled illness to bring this message to FBC's December 2012 gathering at the Clarion. He said: "Emotions make us pay attention right now - this is urgent - and give us an immediate action plan without having to think twice. The emotional component evolved very early: 'Do I eat it, or does it eat me?' You don't sit around and Google it." He added that the emotional response "can take over the rest of the brain in a millisecond, if threatened".

Emotion is a consistent way of responding to the experiences in our lives. It is governed by specific, identifiable brain circuits, and can be measured using objective laboratory methods, such as NFB. Emotion influences the likelihood of feeling particular emotional states, traits, and moods.

The smallest, most fleeting unit of emotion is an emotional state. Typically lasting only a few seconds, it tends to be triggered by an experience - the spike of joy you feel at the macaroni collage which your child made you for Mother's Day; the sense of accomplishment you feel upon finishing a big project at work; the anger you feel over having to work all three days of a holiday weekend;

the sadness you feel when your child is the only one in her class not invited to a party.

Emotional states can also arise from purely mental activity, such as daydreaming, introspection, or anticipating the future. But whether they are triggered by real-world experiences or mental ones, emotional states tend to dissipate, each giving way to the next.

Psychology has been churning out classification schemes with gusto lately - asserting that there are four kinds of temperament, or five components of personality or Lord-knows how many character types. While perfectly interesting and even fun - the popular media have had a field day describing which character types make good romantic matches, business leaders, or psychopaths - these schemes are light on scientific validity, because they are not based on any rigorous analysis of underlying brain mechanisms.

Anything that has to do with human behaviour, feelings, and ways of thinking arises from the brain - so any valid classification scheme must also be based on the brain. That brought me to discover the Emotional Style by Richard J. Davidson, PhD. He stated that Emotional Style comprises of six dimensions.

Neither conventional aspects of personality nor simple emotional traits or moods - let alone diagnostic criteria for mental illness - these six dimensions reflect the discoveries of modern neuroscientific research:

- **Resilience:** How slowly or quickly you recover from adversity.
- **Outlook:** How long you are able to sustain positive emotion.
- **Social Intuition:** How adept you are at picking up social signals from the people around you.
- **Self-Awareness:** How well you perceive bodily feelings that reflect emotions.
- **Sensitivity to Context:** How good you are at regulating your emotional responses to take into account the context you find yourself in.
- **Attention:** How sharp and clear your focus is.

Emotion works with cognition in an integrated and seamless way, to enable us to navigate the world of relationships, work, and spiritual growth. When positive emotion energises us, we are better able to concentrate, to figure out the social networks at a new job or new school, to broaden our thinking so that we can creatively integrate diverse information, and to sustain our interest in a task so we can persevere.

In these cases, emotion is neither interrupting nor disrupting - it is said to be facilitating, which was the main view from the 1970s. A feeling permeates virtually everything we do. It is no wonder, then, that the circuits in the brain which control and regulate emotions overlap with those involved in functions that we think of as being purely cognitive.

The brain signatures of each Emotional Style seem so fundamental to our being, that it is easy to assume they are innate, as characteristic of a person.

Nurture's Effect on Nature

Having a peak performance brain co-exists with having a good heart. If you can self-regulate the relationship between the heart and brain, you will gain positive emotions, coherence, optimal health and cognitive functions.

The billions of neurons in our brains transmit information through electrical and chemical signals. The brain's electrical impulses take the form of waves that researchers categorise by frequency (the number of times they repeat each second). An overabundance or deficiency of one of these frequencies often correlates to conditions such as depression and learning disabilities.

NFB reads these waves, feeds them into a computer and translates them into visual, audible or tactile form. By seeing, hearing or touching your brain waves, you can learn to train your brain to produce desired levels of activity.

There is a growing body of evidence that shows that brain activation has potential benefits for a range of mental health issues, from seizures to learning disabilities right up to substance abuse. Therapists around the world are learning how to change the brain by changing how the brain processes information via its electrical connections.

With today's available technology, NFB helps speed up the process of learning how to meditate, how to quieten and calm the brain - but it does not and cannot replace the brain. Research shows the profound benefits of meditation on the brain, the immune system and the aging process.

NFB has had some remarkable results in dealing with depression, anxiety, sleeping problems, stress, attention issues and autism, amongst others. It makes meditation an option for more people, directly calming the mind by way of giving people a mirror of their actual brain activity at the moment. It's that simple, and yet that profound.

This work has important implications for society, for education, for health and mental health systems, and for the evolution of healthy brain functions itself. The ability to see what our brains are or are not doing at the moment is transformative in and of itself.

Taking Advantage of NFB Peak Performance Training

Many entrepreneurs, leaders, and business owners have started to use NFB peak performance training as part of their leadership development programmes. This is largely due to the recognition that today's business environment has led to:

- Overload, stress and diminished performance, due to relentless productivity demands;
- An erosion in confidence and self-esteem, created by rapidly changing skill requirements and job assignments;
- Increased demand for personal responsibility and accountability, arising from empowerment and emphasis on teams;
- Uncertainty about the balance in work and life, because of the transformation of work through technology; and

- Uncertain in vision, purpose and direction, stemming from discontinuous change.

If today's leaders want to be successful in leading others, they need to be able to handle the additional stress of being a leader. Firstly, they need to become more aware of their stress responses, so that they can work to achieve a level of self-mastery. This will enable them to remain focused in the face of adversity.

NFB ultimately helps leaders, managers, and expert performers to achieve this self-mastery to:

- Clarify and commit to a self-chosen goal;
- Quickly achieve an inner state of calmness and peace in stressful situations;
- Develop an internal sense of control; and
- Cultivate a sense of optimism.

My vision is to develop an Entrepreneur brain.

References

1. James Hopson © 2014 Inspiring Health "Why have I not heard of Neurofeedback before?"
2. Moriyama TS, Polanczyk G, Caye A, Banaschewski T, Brandeis D, Rohde LA (July 2012). "Evidence-based information on the clinical use of neurofeedback for ADHD". *Neurotherapeutics*
3. Lofthouse N, Arnold LE, Hurt E (October 2012). "Current status of neurofeedback for attention-deficit/hyperactivity disorder".
4. Arns M, Hartmut G, Strehl U. "Evaluation of neurofeedback in ADHD: The long and winding road". *Biological Psychology.*
5. Butnik, Steven M. "Neurofeedback in adolescents and adults with attention deficit hyperactivity disorder." *Journal of Clinical Psychology,* May 2005. Vol. 61 Issue 5.
6. Barkley, R. A. & Loo, S. (2005). Clinical utility of EEG in attention deficit hyperactivity disorder. Applied Neuropsychology
7. Lofthouse, N. et al. (2011). A review of neurofeedback treatment for pediatric ADHD. Journal of Attention Disorders, 1087054711427530, first published online November 16, 2011
8. Lofthouse, N. et al. (2011). Biofeedback and neurofeedback treatment for ADHD. Psychiatric Annals
9. Arns, M. et al. (2009). Efficacy of neurofeedback treatment in ADHD. Clinical EEG and Neuroscience
10. Scottish Intercollegiate Guidelines Network (2009). *Management of attention deficit and hyperkinetic disorders in children and young people: A national clinical guideline.* NHS Quality Improvement Scotland. p. 24.
11. Dobie C,; Donald WB, Hanson M, Heim C, Huxsahl J, Karasov R, Kippes C, Neumann A, Spinner P, Staples T, Steiner L. (2012). Diagnosis and Management of Attention Deficit Hyperactivity

Disorder in Primary Care for School-Age Children and Adolescents. Institute for Clinical Systems Improvement. p. 41.

12. Peniston EG, Kulkosky PJ. (1989). "Alpha-theta brainwave training and beta-endorphin levels in alcoholics." *Alcoholism: Clinical and Experimental Research*
13. Bakhshayesh AR, Hänsch S, Wyschkon A, Rezai MJ, Esser G. (2011). "Neurofeedback in ADHD: a single-blind randomized controlled trial." *European Child & Adolescent Psychiatry*
14. Coben R, Linden M, Myers TE. (2010). "Neurofeedback for autistic spectrum disorder: a review of the literature." *Applied Psychophysiology and Biofeedback*
15. Linden DE, Habes I, Johnston SJ, Linden S, Tatineni R, Subramanian L, Sorger B, Healy D, Goebel R. (2012). "Real-time self-regulation of emotion networks in patients with depression."
16. Tan G, Thornby J, Hammond DC, Strehl U, Canady B, Arnemann K, Kaiser DA. (2009). "Meta-analysis of EEG biofeedback in treating epilepsy." *Journal of Clinical EEG & Neuroscience*
17. Jeffrey A. Carmen PhD. (2005). "Passive Infrared Hemoencephalography: Four Years and 100 Migraines." *Journal of Neurotherapy*
18. Cortoos A, De Valck E, Arns M, Breteler MH, Cluydts R. (2010). "An exploratory study on the effects of tele-neurofeedback and tele-biofeedback on objective and subjective sleep in patients with primary insomnia." *Applied Psychophysiology and Biofeedback*
19. Messerotti Benvenuti S, Buodo G, Leone V, Palomba D. (2011). "Neurofeedback training for tourette syndrome: an uncontrolled single case study." *Applied Psychophysiology and Biofeedback*
20. Mihara M, Hattori N, Hatakenaka M, Yagura H, Kawano T, Hino T, Miyai I. (2013). "Near-infrared spectroscopy-mediated neurofeedback enhances efficacy of motor imagery-based training in poststroke victims: a pilot study."
21. Thornton KE, Carmody DP. (208). "Efficacy of traumatic brain injury rehabilitation: interventions of QEEG-guided biofeedback, computers, strategies, and medications." *Applied Psychophysiology and Biofeedback*

22. Marques-Teixeira, F., Sousa, H. & Marques-Teixeira, J. (2013). "Neurofeedback Training for Pure Apathy: a case study." *Iberian Journal of Clinical and Forensic Neuroscience*
23. Egner, Tobias; Gruzelier, John H (1 July 2003). "Ecological validity of neurofeedback". *NeuroReport*
24. Jump up to: ***a b*** Gruzelier, John (1 July 2011). "Neurofeedback and the performing arts." *Neuroscience Letters*
25. Kaiser, David A. "Basic Principles of Quantitative EEG." *Journal of Adult Development*, Vol. 12, Nos. 2/3, August 2005
26. Kamiya, J. (1971). "Operant Control of the EEG Alpha Rhythm and Some of its Reported Effects on Consciousness". *Biofeedback and Self-Control: an Aldine Reader on the Regulation of Bodily Processes and Consciousness.*
27. Frederick, J. (2012). "Psychophysics of EEG Alpha State Discrimination". *Consciousness and Cognition*
28. Hardt, J.V.; Kamiya, J. (1978). "Anxiety change through electroencephalographic alpha feedback seen only in high anxiety subjects". *Science*
29. Paskewitz, D.A.; Orne, M.T. (1973). "Visual Effects on Alpha Feedback Training". *Science*
30. Hardt, J.V.; Kamiya, J. (1976). "Conflicting results in EEG alpha feedback studies". *Applied Psychophysiology and Biofeedback*
31. Clemente, C.D. (1962). "Forebrain inhibitory mechanisms: cortical synchronization induced by basal forebrain stimulation". *Exp Neurol*
32. Sterman, M.B.; Friar, L. (1972). "Suppression of seizures in an epileptic following sensorimotor EEG feedback training". *Electroencephalogr Clin Neurophysiol*
33. Sterman, M.B. (2000). "Basic concepts and clinical findings in the treatment of seizure disorders with EEG operant conditioning". Clin Electroencephalogr
34. Lubar, J.F.; Swartwood, M.O.; Swartwood, J.N.; O'Donnell, P.H. (1995). "Evaluation of the effectiveness of EEG neurofeedback training for ADHD in a clinical setting as measured by changes in TOVA

scores, behavioral ratings, and WISC-R performance". Applied Psychophysiology and Biofeedback

35. Levesque, Johanne and Mario Beauregard. "Effect of neurofeedback training on the neural substrates of selective attention in children with attention-deficit/hyperactivity disorder: A functional magnetic resonance imaging study." Neuroscience Letters,
36. http://www.neurofeedback-scotland.com/alpha-theta-brainwave.html
37. http://www.neurofeedback-scotland.com/anxiety-disorders.html
38. Thornton, K. & Carmody, D. Eyes-Closed and Activation QEEG Databases in Predicting Cognitive Effectiveness and the Inefficiency Hypothesis, Journal of Neurotherapy, 2009
39. http://www.bfe.org/
40. Neblett, R., Shaffer, F., & Crawford, J. (2008). What is the value of Biofeedback Certification Institute of America certification? Biofeedback
41. Washington State Legislature WAC 296-21-280 Biofeedback Rules.
42. Gevirtz, R. (2003). The behavioral health provider in mind-body medicine. In D. Moss, A. McGrady, T. C. Davies, & I. Wickramasekera (Eds.). Handbook of mind-body medicine for primary care. Thousand Oaks, CA: Sage Publications, Inc.
43. De Bease, C. (2007). Biofeedback Certification Institute of America certification: Building skills without walls. Biofeedback, 35(2), 48-49.
44. Shaffer, F., & Schwartz, M. S. (in press). Entering the field and assuring competence. In M. S. Schwartz, & F. Andrasik (Eds.). Biofeedback: A practitioner's guide (4th ed.). New York: The Guilford Press.
45. Ros T.; Munneke M.A.M., Ruge D., Gruzelier J.H., Rothwell J.C. (2010). "Endogenous Control of Waking Brain Rhythms Induces Neuroplasticity in Humans". European Journal of Neuroscience
46. Health.howstuffworks.com/mental-health/adhd/adhd-and-neuro feedback.htm
47. www.aboutneurofeedback.com/neurofeedback-info-center/faq/
48. www.additudemag.com>home>ADHD>treatment>Alternative
49. www.brainandhealth.com/
50. www.centerforbrain.com/condition

51. www.eeginfo.com/../epilepsy_main.php
52. Sharon Tenenbaum "How these inherent and artistic rules of the subconscious mind affect our visual interpretation of art." Sept 2013
53. Tania Lombrozo "The Truth About The Left Brain / Right Brain Relationship" December 02, 2013
54. http://www.ipn.at
55. Griggs, Richard A. Psychology: A Concise Introduction. p. 69.
56. Nielsen, Jared A., Brandon A. Zielinski, Michael A. Ferguson, Janet E. Lainhart, and Jeffrey S. Anderson. "An Evaluation of the Left-Brain vs. Right-Brain Hypothesis with Resting State Functional Connectivity Magnetic Resonance Imaging." PLOS ONE, 14 Aug. 2013. Web. 30 Aug. 2013.
57. Westen et al. 2006 Psychology: Australian and New Zealand edition. John Wiley p.107
58. Toga, A. W.; Thompson, P. M. (2003). "Mapping brain asymmetry". Nature Reviews Neuroscience
59. Pulsifer, M. B.; Brandt, J.; Salorio, C. F.; Vining, E. P.; Carson, B. S.; Freeman, J. M. (2004). "The cognitive outcome of hemispherectomy in 71 children". Epilepsia
60. Knecht, S.; Dräger, B.; Deppe, M.; Bobe, L.; Lohmann, H.; Flöel, A.; Ringelstein, E. B.; Henningsen, H. (2000). "Handedness and hemispheric language dominance in healthy humans". Brain: a journal of neurology
61. Schönwiesner, M.; Rübsamen, R.; Von Cramon, D. Y. (2005). "Hemispheric asymmetry for spectral and temporal processing in the human antero-lateral auditory belt cortex". European Journal of Neuroscience
62. Taylor, Insep and Taylor, M. Martin (1990) "Psycholinguistics: Learning and using Language". page 362
63. Regarding different languages: http://www.bbc.co.uk/news/health-11181457
64. Goswami U (2006). "Neuroscience and education: from research to practice?". Nat Rev Neurosci

65. Kandel E, Schwartz J, Jessel T. Principles of Neural Science. 4th ed. p1182. New York: McGraw–Hill; 2000.
66. Maccoby, Eleanor (1974). The Psychology of Sex Differences. Stanford, California: Stanford University Press. ISBN 0804709742.
67. Dardo Tomasi, Nora D. Volkow (June 2012). "Laterality Patterns of Brain Functional Connectivity: Gender Effects". Cerebral Cortex
68. Boeree, C.G. (2004). "Speech and the Brain". Retrieved February 17, 2012.
69. Taylor, I. & Taylor, M. M. (1990). Psycholinguistics: Learning and using Language. Pearson. ISBN 978-0-13-733817-7. p. 367
70. Beaumont, J.G. (2008). Introduction to Neuropsychology, Second Edition. The Guilford Press. ISBN 978-1-59385-068-5. Chapter 7
71. Ross ED, Monnot M (January 2008). "Neurology of affective prosody and its functional-anatomic organization in right hemisphere". Brain Lang.
72. George MS, Parekh PI, Rosinsky N, Ketter TA, Kimbrell TA, Heilman KM, Herscovitch P, Post RM (July 1996). "Understanding Emotional Prosody Activates Right Hemisphere Regions". Arch Neurol.
73. Dehaene S, Spelke E, Pinel P, Stanescu R, Tsivkin S (May 1999). "Sources of mathematical thinking: behavioral and brain-imaging evidence".
74. Dehaene, S., Piazza, M., Pinel, P. & Cohen, L. (2003). "Three parietal circuits for number processing". Cognitive Neuropsychology
75. Levy LM, Reis IL, Grafman J (August 1999). "Metabolic abnormalities detected by 1H-MRS in dyscalculia and dysgraphia". Neurology
76. Hecht D (October 2010). "Depression and the hyperactive right-hemisphere". Neurosci. Res.
77. Braun CM, Delisle J, Guimond A, Daigneault R (March 2009). "Post unilateral lesion response biases modulate memory: crossed double dissociation of hemispheric specialisations". Laterality
78. Devinsky O (January 2009). "Delusional misidentifications and duplications: right brain lesions, left brain delusions". Neurology
79. Madoz-Gúrpide A, Hillers-Rodríguez R (April 2010). "[Capgras delusion: a review of aetiological theories]". Rev Neurol 50

80. Goldberg, E. (2009). The New Executive Brain: Frontal Lobes in a Complex World. New York, NY: Oxford University Press. ISBN 978-0-19-532940-7.
81. Knecht, S.; Dräger, B.; Deppe, M.; Bobe, L.; Lohmann, H.; Flöel, A.; Ringelstein, E. B.; Henningsen, H. (2000). "Handedness and hemispheric language dominance in healthy humans". Brain 123
82. Hines, Terence (1987). "Left Brain/Right Brain Mythology and Implications for Management and Training". The Academy of Management Review 12
83. Drenth, J. D. (2003). "Growing anti-intellectualism in Europe; a menace to science". Studia Psychologica 45 available in ALLEA Annual Report 2003, pp. 61–72
84. Sala, Sergio Della (1999). Mind Myths: Exploring Popular Assumptions about the Mind and Brain. New York: Wiley. ISBN 0-471-98303-9.
85. Vallortigara, G.; Rogers, L. J. (2005). "Survival with an asymmetrical brain: Advantages and disadvantages of cerebral lateralization". Behavioral and Brain Sciences 28
86. Halpern et al. (2005). "Lateralization of the Vertebrate Brain: Taking the Side of Model Systems". The Journal of Neuroscience 25
87. Rogers (1990). "Light Input and the Reversal of Functional Lateralization in the Chicken Brain". Behav Brain Res 38
88. Deng, Rogers (1997). "Differential Contributions of the Two Visual Pathways to Functional Lateralization in Chicks". Behav Brain Res 87
89. Rogers (2000). "Evolution of Hemispheric Specialization: Advantages and Disadvantages". Brain Lang 73
90. Pam Zhang "Meditation's Effects on Alpha Brain Waves" January 15, 2014
91. www.brainworksneurotherapy.com/ what are brainwaves
92. www.brainandhealth.com/brainwaves
93. Carol Sorgen, WebMD Feature. Reviewed by Louise Chang, MD "Eat Smart for a Healthier Brain Add these 'superfoods' to your daily diet, and you will increase your odds of maintaining a healthy brain for the rest of your life." @www.webmd.com

94. Nadler, R. (2009) "What was I thinking? Handling the Hijack." November 21, 2012:
95. Goleman, D. (2004) "What makes a leader?" November 21, 2012
96. Horowitz, S. "Emotional Intelligence - Stop Amygdala Hijackings." November 21, 2012.
97. Goulston M.D., Mark (2009-09-15). Just Listen: Discover the Secret to Getting Through to Absolutely Anyone
98. Davidson, Richard J. (2012). The Emotional Life of Your Brain: How Its Unique Patterns Affect the Way You Think, Feel, and Live - and How You Can Change Them

THE DICKSON LAB

The Dickson Lab is a multidisciplinary space that brings objective scientific tools and techniques together with subjective inner knowing to accelerate human potential. Founded with an ambitious vision to make the uncommon sense common in the society by leveraging on practical, sensible knowledge and technologies while working along with several highly functioning individuals and organizations who are clear leaders in all their respective arenas.

WEBSITE
www.TheDicksonLab.com

E-MAIL
Dickson@DicksonLab.com

■ EMOWAVE ■

A person's voice is the blueprint to their emotional intelligence. As we speak, our vocal chords appear to link with our emotinal state. EmoWave™ is a technology that performs a voice analysis which in turn, enables possibility of performing further analysis as needed or wanted. It was designed in a matrix format that covers several dimensions in the area of:

- Emotional Stress Level.
- Emotional Intelligence Blueprint.
- Learning & Communication Style.
- Characteristics and Your Real Intention.
- Mental & Physical wellness.

EmoWave™

The 1st Profiling Tool That Measure Emotional Intelligence.

EmoPill™

The brain's auditory receptors connect with the prescribed frequency sent via the customized EmoPill™, it will engage the brain to potentially create the state needed to help the person move towards the desire outcome. By listening to the customized EmoPill™ on a daily basis, the individual can potentially enhance positive emotional intelligence attributes and neutralize or possibly even eliminate negative emotional consequences.

COACHING WITH FACTS

Differentiate between Opinions and Facts. The coach will discover your strengths and weakness, the trueness inside of you. He will provides structure, guidance, support and accountability designed to create positive change in personal, career or even business behaviour.

Printed in the United States
By Bookmasters